To Adena - a
with, richness
resiliency).
Thanks for, the generous
support!
Love,
Lisa

RESILIENCY:

How To Bounce Back
Faster, Stronger, Smarter

RESILIENCY:

How To Bounce Back
Faster, Stronger, Smarter

By Tessa Albert Warschaw, Ph.D.
& Dee Barlow, Ph.D.

HERITAGE
IMPRINT

MASTER MEDIA Ltd. • New York, NY

All rights reserved, including the right of
reproduction in whole or in part in any form.
Published by MasterMedia Limited.

MASTERMEDIA and colophon are registered trademarks
of MasterMedia Limited

Library of Congress Catalog Card Number: 95-078077

ISBN 1-57101-021-1

Interior design by Lisa L. Cangemi
First Printing October 1995
Manufactured in the United States of America
10 9 8 7 6 5 4 3 2 1

Dedication

To my mother, Ann,
whose resiliency continues
to inspire me day-by-day
and
to my husband, Sam,
whose *Joie de Vivre* nourishes my spirit
and enhances my resiliency.

Tessa Albert Warschaw

To my mother, Ann,
whose determination to live forever
belies the delicacy of her southern beauty.
And to my unfailingly optimistic
and committed husband, Richard,
whose faith, integrity, imagination,
and collaborative nature
provided my model for this book.

Dee Barlow

✴ CONTENTS ✴

PART 1 - Resiliency: What It Is, What It Isn't, Who Has It

Chapter 1 — Resiliency Defined • 1

Chapter 2 — Natural Resiliency • 8

Chapter 3 — Learned Resiliency • 15

PART 2 - Resiliency: Working On It

Chapter 4 — Getting It Into Perspective • 24

Chapter 5 — Authenticity and Conscience • 35

Chapter 6 — Imagination and Hope • 46

Chapter 7 — Negotiating and Collaboration • 60

Chapter 8 — Finding Your Collaborative Style • 72

PART 3 - Resiliency Quotient: Checking It Out

Chapter 9 — RQ Questionnaire • 86

PART 4 - Bouncing Back Faster, Stronger, Smarter

Chapter 10 — Bouncing Back Faster: Getting Started • 94

Chapter 11 — Bouncing Back Stronger: Keeping It Going • 111

Chapter 12 — Bouncing Back Smarter:
Going To The Next Level • 126

Chapter 13 — Bouncing Back Step By Step:
The Serious Stuff Of Life • 137

PART 5 - The Spiritual Connection

Chapter 14 — The Responsibility Of Choosing • 158

Have you had your change today?

The only constant in life is change. Even the happy changes create some adjustment problems. The long awaited birth of a healthy baby, for example, or getting that big promotion have stress side effects. How much more stressful is losing the baby through miscarriage or failing to get the promotion?

As therapists and organizational consultants, we work every day with people who are having difficulty recovering from negative changes or the negative results of change, from setbacks — whether that setback be a divorce or a disappointment, an illness or a failed hope, bad luck or a bad ending, a loss of money or reputation or love, or a natural disaster or death. Almost no one has the luxury of a slow recovery, of wallowing in life's defeats. Who can spend more than a weekend in bed with the remote control before having to get back out there into the game?

Never has the ability to bounce back been more important, because the speed of change today is faster than it ever was and the pressure to produce and succeed more intense. We are, in fact, bombarded by change — in technology, science and medicine, the configuration of world politics and office politics, social mores, and the economics of our personal lives. The information explosion, which keeps track of these changes, makes many people anxious, pushes some into withdrawal, and creates in nearly all of us a pervasive sense of fear of the future. How much more change will we have to endure? And how will we cope?

In the early 1960s, Alvin Toeffler warned in the book, *Future Shock*, of our increasing need to adapt to change on an individual level. More recently Thomas Kuhn, in *The Structure of Scientific Revolutions*, described "paradigm shifts," dramatic shifts in how we think and behave and perceive the world around us. Increasingly we feel the need to prepare for a future which we can scarcely imagine in any detail.

Who would have thought twenty-five years ago that fax machines, VCRs, home computers, and microwaves would be standard appliances in the middle-class home? And who would have guessed that approximately one-third of all adult males between the ages of 26 and 34 would be living with their parents as they are today? The past is no longer the trusted guide it once was. At the same time people are feeling increasingly adrift in the world, they long for a sense of spirituality in their lives - for the rediscovery of that animating principal in each of us that makes sense of living in a senseless world.

Ironically, just at the point in history where people need to bounce back faster, stronger, and smarter than at any other time, they are losing their ability to do so. The people we see are finding it harder and harder to recover from a setback, to bounce back from the blows that life inevitably has in store for each of us. This is true for people from all socioeconomic levels and all geographic locales - from the fired executive to the man or woman whose spouse has left them for someone else.

Anxiety and fearfulness about the future cause some people to lead constricted lives. They become entrenched in their setback positions and don't move forward from a defeat or a mistake because they are afraid of experiencing another defeat, making another mistake. Sadly, they have abandoned the pursuit of excellence as a goal because that goal demands that they take risks which will probably lead them to fail again before they can succeed.

"Show me a man that is not making mistakes and I will show you a man that is not learning anything," Buckminster Fuller once said.

Learning from mistakes and recovering from setbacks as fast as possible require the quality of resiliency.

What Is resiliency?

There is a wonderful quality within people that we call resiliency, which allows them to bounce back from physical and psychological traumas. Resiliency enabled some survivors of the Holocaust to walk out of concentration camps and lead vital, productive lives. And it allows some victims of war or child abuse or other forms of repetitive violence — including the daily assault of verbal abuse — to believe in love and goodness though they have seen much hate and evil.

Resilient people are energetically engaged with life. The strength of this engagement makes them resistant to giving up in the face of problems or setbacks which might seem overwhelming to someone who is not resilient. The core of resiliency is an unambivalent commitment to life. Whether their faith comes from a belief in God or higher power or love of mankind and nature, they enthusiastically embrace life.

Personal resiliency makes the difference in whether you bounce back when fate knocks you down — or lie there on the mat.

Why resiliency?

If you're alive, you need resiliency.

No life is without setbacks, disappointments, failures. Some lives seem to have more than their fair share of them. The more bad cards in your hand, the greater is your need for resiliency. A lot of good cards — an overload of positives — can create problems, too. If everything starts going your way at once, you must be resilient to handle the onslaught of changes.

Robert Louis Stevenson said, "Life is not a matter of holding good cards but of playing a poor hand well."

If you want to achieve your personal goals, cope with personal and professional transitions, grow with your spouse, friends, and family, love and be loved, and comeback from setbacks - you need resiliency.

Especially now, you need resiliency. The skills we need to survive and succeed in the world today bear little relation to the skills our parents needed. And the skills our children will need in another twenty-five years will probably be equally remote from the ones required today. In a world where disconnection, dislocation, and disorganization seem prevalent, you need to be resilient.

Who Has resiliency?

Some people seem to be born with it. They develop resiliency in earliest infancy due to inborn traits and/or a good bonding experience with a caregiver. These people bounce back from setbacks — often growing stronger and smarter in the process.

But we strongly believe that less resilient people can learn the habits, attitudes, and skills that allow the quality to develop. We have seen this happen in our work as therapists and consultants. With guidance, information, positive support, and encouragement, less resilient people can increase their commitment to life - and their resiliency.

Can you become more resilient?

Yes, you can. Other people have done so. Why not you?

Throughout this book, we are going to show you how to become more resilient in your personal and professional lives. We'll teach you the skills for bouncing back from the everyday stresses that are not overwhelming yet occupy most of our time, to the skills needed for surviving disastrous multiple losses. And, through the inspiring stories of others, you will see that the unambivalent commitment to life which is the core of resiliency is a commitment you can't afford not to make.

PART ONE

RESILIENCY:
WHAT IT IS,
WHAT IT ISN'T,
WHO HAS IT

CHAPTER ONE

RESILIENCY DEFINED

When we asked Amber Brookman the definition of resiliency, she said, "MYSELF! I am like a ram who keeps butting up against the wall and even when I am down I stand up and do it again. I use my anger whenever I am told, 'You can't.' I know I CAN do it!"

The Chief Executive Officer of Brookwood Companies, Brookman, a former model, took this bankrupt textile business in a male-dominated industry and turned it into a flourishing company. That is only the most recent of her many astounding accomplishments. Articulate, slender, beautiful, and generous, she has bounced back from two divorces, raised a child (Amber, Jr.) alone, and survived the tough Los Angeles and New York City modeling industry. She invested at age twenty-two in her first piece of property - for which she paid $135.00 in monthly payments of $22.00. Today her real estate portfolio has included vacant land, single-family residences, a New York apartment, and a multifamily apartment building - in addition to her own lovely home with tennis court and pool.

She has known her share of "downs" — but she always came back "up," higher and higher than she'd been before. "When the world is falling apart, I get turned on to crisis! I enjoy crisis management."

"From every low point, I looked up," she says. "In my heart, I always knew I was ready for the next episode and could face it head on, whatever it was. And I was always ready to prove wrong the people who said I couldn't do whatever it was I wanted to do.

"When someone said to me, 'What makes you think you can do that?' — I had to show them I could. 'What makes you think you can succeed in business when you never went to college?' people asked me. She laughs. I remember when someone asked me, 'What makes you think you can own property when you have no money to invest?' I KNEW I could!

"I run toward success with wide open arms."

The resiliency components

In science, resiliency is the power or ability of a substance to return to its original form after being bent or stretched or twisted or pushed or pulled. Resilient people, like Amber Brookman, have that same power or ability. Life's challenges may bend and stretch and twist them. Other people may relentlessly push and pull them. They bounce back faster, stronger, smarter.

Resilient people have patterns of response, which include emotional, attitudinal, and behavioral components. These components are the conditioned "muscles" of resiliency. Like athletes who get second or third "winds" which carry them through a long run or a competition, resilient people bounce back from setbacks without needing a serious time-out to worry, be fearful or angry, or, especially, to agonize over whether they really want to come back at all. They do it because they have an unambivalent commitment to life which never has to be renegotiated or reconsidered. They do it because they never consider not doing it.

As one resilient man told us, "I believe the cornerstone of my resiliency is my indomitable curiosity and my belief in the future. I cannot contain it."

The ten components of resiliency:

• *Unambivalent Commitment to Life.* We cannot stress this enough. The common core of resilient people is this transcendent attitude or belief which gives them the passion and courage to bounce back. They don't waste time agonizing over whether or not life is worth living. They know: It is.

• *Self-confidence.* Resilient people believe they can understand the world around them, set realistic goals to achieve in that world, and develop the skills required for doing so. This confidence gives them the strength to strive for their aspirations while retaining a sense of integrity. With such a positive mental attitude, they see problems and changes as opportunities for growth and learning, rather than threats or burdens to be avoided or shifted to someone else.

• *Adaptability.* Adaptable people can modify their habits to work with others, both personally and professionally. They tend to be cooperative people who elicit helpful responses from family, friends, and coworkers. Often they are actively engaged in championing the rights of others.

• *Resourcefulness.* Resilient people know what resources are available for problem solving and where they can turn for support when they must have it. They know where and how to find the help they need - even if they don't need it often - from family, friends, co-workers, educational and spiritual institutions. And they are creative and imaginative in the way they use resources to solve problems. In fact, they spend much of their life building and accumulating these varied resources. They don't have only one friend or one career interest.

• *Willingness to Risk.* It isn't always possible to know the outcome of an action or a behavior, particularly in complex situations. Sometimes an action or a decision is a risk for that reason. The resilient person doesn't always play it "safe" but takes intelligent risks grounded in real possibilities and with a good chance for success.

• *Acceptance of Personal Responsibility.* Resilient people have a strong philosophical or spiritual belief in self-determination. If deeply religious, they believe that God imposes the responsibility to choose their destiny and actively make His work their own. They are unwilling to claim victim status. And, they don't make excuses when they make mistakes. By owning their mistakes, they turn them into positive learning experiences.

• *Perspective.* Resilient people know what is important and what is not. They put their energy into serious or core issues and activities and dismiss - or enjoy - the inconsequential ones. Most often, they have a good sense of humor and even know how to use humor as a strategic tool in alleviating pain and tension in serious situations.

• *Openness to New Ideas.* They take in new information eagerly - and without excessive prejudgment. Free of the rigidity which accompanies a narrow outlook on life, they investigate and evaluate new information, sorting and storing for the future. They don't close their minds to anything that would increase their capacity to learn and adapt.

• *Willingness to Be Proactive.* Resiliency is proactive — rather than reactive. Resilient people meet challenge with positive action rather than waiting until the only recourse possible is a reaction to actions already taken by others. They aren't stopped cold by fear of the unknown, confusion, inflexible beliefs, or the conviction that "nothing can be done." Rather, they are action-oriented.

• *Attentiveness.* They are paying attention to the world around them. When you speak to them, they are listening. Resilient people don't shut out other voices and form a plan of action which doesn't take into consideration any perspective or reality but their own.

Do resilient people sail through life?

Resiliency is not a magic carpet. Resilient people can find the process of growth and learning an uncomfortable one at times. But they are willing to be uncomfortable for a short time to achieve their long-term goals.

Resilient people are not immune to stress. We have observed that they seem to possess the skills of pacing and timing to a far greater degree than non-resilient people. Like the long-distance runner, they pace themselves to avoid burn-out. We call this pacing and timing process "leveraging resiliency." By leveraging your resiliency — or measuring and allocating your time, energy, and resources rather than exhausting them in frantic bursts — you create more resiliency. Failure to leverage your resiliency and maintain balance in your life leads to burn out. And what is burn out if not a loss of resiliency?

What resiliency isn't

The war hero is definitely a survivor, but he may or may not be resilient. The battered wife who finally leaves her husband, the verbally battered victim of corporate downsizing who lands in a good job in a competing company, the earthquake victim who rebuilds after losing everything — they are all survivors. But are they resilient? And what about the woman you see at a party whose effervescence belies recent personal tragedies or that couple who have risked everything they own on a precarious business venture? Resilient or not?

On the surface, some people look like they have the quality when they really don't. The soldier may have thought of little else but death in the prison camp. The ebullient partygoer may fuel her spirits with alcohol or drugs, which leave her feeling empty and desperate when the evening is over. And the couple who risked everything may believe in nothing at all.

Resiliency is not:

• *Survival.* It isn't just survival. Survival is often misread as resiliency. Many people survive natural disasters, career upheaval, divorce, and other personal disasters without being resilient. They may look fine on the outside, but inside they are not doing well. Rarely free of their past baggage, they do not have that critical unambivalent commitment to life. Weighed down psychologically and often physically by their hurts, pains, disappointments, and suffering - they are ambivalent about life.

• *Reckless Behavior.* Actions which are likely to lead to loss may look like planned risk-taking, but the reckless person has much in common with someone who takes no risks at all and simply hides out in fear of life. Both make loss inevitable by the way they manage risk.

• *Dwelling in the Past.* Spending a lot of time in the past is nonresilient behavior, even if the time is spent in an attempt to analyze or understand that past. (Assessing the past is a useful tool when it is undertaken as a means of understanding the present and positively influencing the future.) In fact, a core difference between resilient people and nonresilient people is their attitude toward the past. The resilient person looks to the future, the nonresilient person to the past. Future orientation is inherently pragmatic and requires imagination. Dwelling in the past leads to stagnation.

• *Aimless Pleasure Seeking.* All around us people are going to extremes for stimulation or pleasure. Much of their hunger for stimulation through addictive substances or dangerous behaviors, even pain, is a real longing for deep feeling. Alienated from their deepest values, desires, and feelings, they use drugs, sex, violence, acquisition and hoarding to fill the emptiness and still the anxiety. From the outside, they may look like people who can cope with any situation — but nothing could be further from the truth.

Resiliency is grounded in reality, not the guise of reality. It offers real substance, real pleasure, real satisfaction, real growth. Without that grounding in reality, there is no hope.

Do you really need resiliency?

You can't bounce back without it. And most of us do want to lead vital, productive lives. We want to face challenges with the hope that we can do more than survive them. Yes, we want to bounce back.

"Take hope from the heart of man and you make him a beast of prey," said the English novelist, Ouida.

Resiliency is full of hope. The absence of it is hopelessness. When you choose to build the skills and practice the behaviors that will help you bounce back from setbacks, you are choosing life. Don't wait until you have been knocked down to decide that you want to come back up faster, stronger and smarter than you ever were. Make that choice now.

You can't be resilient at the last moment if your habits haven't encouraged resiliency before. The disciplined muscle responds automatically. The unused muscle probably can't lift you up without becoming strained. Resiliency breeds resiliency — for those who add discipline to their conviction and commitment to life.

CHAPTER TWO

NATURAL RESILIENCY

"**I** was born in Washington D. C., and from the ages of six weeks to twelve years was shifted back and forth between the city and my aunt's farm in a small rural Maryland community," says Bobbie Jordan, a teacher and lecturer. "My Aunt Louise took me to church at the age of six weeks. I was on the 'Cradle Roll.' She was a truly good Christian woman and practiced her faith daily in her home. Her values were honesty, compassion, and hard work. She saw to it that I was able to attend Vacation Bible School every summer until I was twelve years old."

Jordan's mother suffered from ill health but nevertheless worked long hours as a nurse. When she was twelve, her parents decided she and her sister should stay full time with them. That move was like going from "heaven," the country, to "hell," the city.

"I practically raised my sister," she says. "And I did all of the washing, ironing, food preparation and house cleaning. No matter how hard I tried, nothing I did was ever good enough for my father. He never physically abused either my sister or me, but the curse words flew and the condemnations landed almost daily for one trivial or imagined fault after another.

"When I was fourteen, my mother decided I should be allowed to live with another aunt if I wanted to. From that day on, my whole outlook on life changed. My aunt's husband had died three months earlier and she was as in need of me as I was of her."

Her aunt encouraged her interest in reading and learning. When Jordan came home from school one day in tears over a difficult assignment, her aunt said, "There is not one other person in that class who is any smarter than you are. You will always be able to do just what you think you can do."

Today Bobbie Jordan lectures for the College Board to advanced placement teachers across the country and presents workshops during the summer months.

"My basic resiliency and commitment to life was modeled after my aunts who gave me strength, confidence, and faith — and my mother, who was patient, sacrificing and loving," Jordan says.

What is natural resiliency?

Some people seem to possess resiliency from birth - or at least from childhood. There may be nothing in their environment or background to explain why they are "vulnerable but invincible," in the words of E. E. Werner and R. S. Smith who studied resiliency in children. They may have come from impoverished backgrounds or suffered neglect or abuse - or, like Bobbie Jordan, moved from one home to another and had to assume family responsibilities at a very early age. What then are the inherent attributes that contribute to this early development of resiliency?

• A sense of commitment and meaning that gives the child a feeling of control and "coherence".

• Intelligence and a positive disposition that elicits helpful responses from others. It makes sense that a child who is gifted with intelligence would have a better chance of seeing possibilities when confronted with challenges. And a socially adept child would have a better chance of handling stress than a nervous, high-strung, or easily agitated child.

• A proactive problem-solving style. When confronted with challenges, they assume responsibility and look for solutions. The child who independently figures out how the new toy's pieces fit together is proactive - independent rather than dependent. Rather than giving up in frustration or crying until an adult shows him how to make the toy work, he begins to solve the problem himself.

• Adaptability. The child has a largely positive attitude toward change and deals confidently with new, even troubling situations. Anger and fear seem to be used as spurs to deal with adversity.

Even a child with a lackluster mind or an overactive disposition can acquire resiliency through the early nurturing of one consistent caregiver. Repeatedly the presence of this one supportive person has been highlighted by psychologists as "the saving grace" that made the difference in the child's life. Resilient children develop a sense of self and make commitments very early, forming ready bonds with other children and caregivers, with pets, favorite teachers, toys, and activities they enjoy. Whether early resiliency is a result of the inherent attributes or learned through the support of a caring adult — or both — the results are noticeable in even the youngest child.

What does natural resiliency look like?

"On reflection, no one — least of all her Mom — is surprised that even as a toddler, Julie Krone seemed to know instinctively what to do on a moving horse," write Lindsey Johnson and Jackie Joyner-Kersee in *A Woman's Place Is Everywhere.* "Maybe it was because her mother had ridden throughout her pregnancy; even in the womb, little Julie had felt the rhythm of horses."

Years later, Krone would observe, "I was always going to be a jockey - and a great one, too."

Now at age thirty, Julie Krone is indeed the most successful female jockey in the history of horse racing. She's been thrown down, stomped on, and sideswiped by other jockeys. But somehow Krone never fails to get up, dust herself off, and get back on the horse. Even a devastating fall didn't dampen her spirits for long. After a few weeks in the hospital, Krone was flying around in her wheelchair, whipping her crop like she was riding a filly into the stretch.

"When something you do, something you live for, is yanked away and you're in the dark, you reach for God, religion, family," Julie said.

Julie Krone's indomitability is apparent in her story of physical courage and spiritual triumph, but most resilient people live quieter lives, their own brand of courage less dramatic than hers.

A typical American family

If any family could be described as "normal" and "healthy," it is the Maginns of Omaha, Nebraska. John Maginn, age fifty-five, is the senior executive vice president, chief investment officer, and treasurer of a large financial institution. His wife, Carol, has owned and operated her own successful retail business *As You Like It* for fifteen years. Devout Catholics, they have raised four children while managing two careers and taking an active part in their large extended families. No one in the nuclear family is overweight or visibly stressed or underachieving. There are no drug and alcohol problems. There is no lack of good humor, broad-mindedness, kindness and adventuresome spirit in this family, either.

How did the Maginns become so resilient?

Don't write this off as their choice of geography. "Who couldn't pull it off in Omaha?" groused a corporate executive in Manhattan. Many people can't pull it off in Omaha or in any other town or city you name. Every small town, medium-sized city, and rural area in this country has its fair share of crime, alcoholism, drug abuse — and alienated, rebellious young people. Geography is not the answer.

John, the eldest of three siblings, credits his large family, supportive friends, and especially, the philosophy of life he learned from his father for helping him develop resiliency.

"My father, Walt, was my role model," he says. "He was the humblest man I ever knew. He grew up poor during the Great Depression and worked with his father on the family farm."

With only a high school diploma, he rose to the position of director and senior financial officer with the same corporation John joined after graduating with a master's degree from the University of Minnesota.

"His ascendancy was due to his immense common sense, his responsibility, and his work ethic," John says. "Despite suffering serious health problems requiring several surgeries from age thirty-nine until his death from a heart attack at the age of fifty-eight, he was still working when he died."

Walt's health problems, which began in John's fourteenth year, and the way he handled them, shaped his son's life.

"I remember a lot of time spent sitting by my father's bedside," John says. "We had a good relationship in his healthy years, but we developed a closeness during his illnesses that might not have happened otherwise. He continued to be an active father to me even from his hospital bed, because he believed a man should never neglect his family — or his work. My father endured great pain and suffering without complaint or self-pity - or asking, 'Why me?'"

John's mother, who was strong and healthy, also contributed to his development of resiliency. An outgoing and generous woman, she sacrificed for her family without complaining. John remembers his parents' marriage as "filled with love, respect, and affection." When he met his wife, Carol, in college, he recognized that she was the woman with whom he could share that kind of marriage.

"After I'd introduced her to my parents, they told me, 'Don't let that young lady get away!'" he says. "I didn't."

Obviously, John had many of the advantages associated with the early and natural development of resiliency: a happy family, a strong religious foundation, a stable community, a good education. Our belief, however, is that his great admiration, love, and respect for his parents was the greatest asset in his life.

Listen to John's description of his philosophy of life and the sources of his resiliency:

"I rely on my maternal grandfather's advice: 'Take each day as it comes, do your best, and resolve each evening to get up the next morning and try even harder.'

"I always turn to prayer, particularly to help me understand my own accountability for my actions.

"I recognize that every crisis embodies danger and opportunity. I try to make sure I understand the danger and focus mostly on the opportunity.

"Looking to the example set by my father, I try to accept success or failure with grace, ease, and humility. I also try to be without pride or self-pity. I realize that life is a mystery to be lived, not a problem to be solved, and that this life is only one part of my existence.

"I believe that life is not simple or easy. God does not set us up to fail, but He does give us the strength to endure and the wisdom to determine, understand, and accept. I try to live my life in a manner that is pleasing to my God, who is a living, loving, and compassionate God.

"I see myself as a resource, serving at the pleasure of others and striving to make a positive and valued contribution as a token of my appreciation.

"I never give up on myself or take things too seriously or personally. I understand there are always worse things in life and people who are far worse off than I am."

Three portraits - Three models

Bobbie Jordan, Julie Krone, and John Maginn are three quite different examples of natural resiliency.

Jordan bounced back from the kind of childhood traumas others use as excuses for their failure to accomplish their goals as adults. Rather than wasting her time blaming her father for not providing the nurturing she needed, she is grateful to her mother and aunts because they did. She gained self-confidence from meeting repeated early challenges.

Krone exhibits an almost defiant, "in your face" resiliency. Her recovery from a dreadful accident is only partly a physical triumph. Yes, the body was mended. Watching a grimace of pain cross her face as she determinedly gets back in the saddle, you would have to conclude it is her spirit that carried her back to the racetrack.

There is little drama in the daily life of John Maginn who quietly, steadily works at his job and loves his family. His personal philosophy gives meaning to everything he does, no matter how mundane those activities may seem. Bobbie, Julie, and John are good models of resiliency. Their styles may differ widely, but their lives offer lessons for all of us.

It is our belief that resiliency is learned very early by some and later in life by others. If you didn't learn it early, you can still develop it throughout your lifetime. There are many ways of doing that — as we'll show you in the chapters ahead.

CHAPTER THREE

LEARNED RESILIENCY

"**M**y mother died in childbirth, leaving my father to raise me and two younger sisters," Jane Weston says. "He was strict and demanding. I became the mother to my sisters and the homemaker for all of us. My father had rigid beliefs about what one could accomplish in life. His ambitions for me were limited to cooking, cleaning, caring for the family. I was not to aspire to more than that."

Luckily, a teacher saw Weston's potential and encouraged her to go away to college. Away from her demanding father, she succeeded in school and later in her career in New York City where she eventually became the first woman vice president of a manufacturing company.

"In early adulthood, I went through a compliant period," she says, "where I tried to please bosses and lovers the way I had strived to please my father. But that teacher had instilled in me a lifetime passion for learning. I used every mechanism for self-learning available — videos, audios, seminars, you name it. The more information I absorbed, the more confident — and less compliant — I became."

Weston kept pressing forward. She suffered the routine setbacks of employment, including being fired, but she bounced back each time by applying herself to the process of learning.

"I am a true believer in the maxim that nothing is impossible," she says — a lesson she credits to the teacher who encouraged her in high school.

What is learned resiliency?

Jane Weston is a good example of learned resiliency. Many fortunate people experience love and security in infancy and have abundant resources in childhood. Others have severe injuries — emotional, mental, or physical — or suffer losses in infancy and childhood, but learn resiliency from a nurturing caregiver. Weston got started on the path to resiliency in late adolescence with her teacher's interest in her, which was like a spark igniting her spirit inside. She was an adult before she truly began to feel confident — and resilient.

People are capable of becoming more resilient as they experience challenges and setbacks, but this is certainly not an automatic process.

How you handle loss, injury, grief, challenge — even positive changes — determines whether or not you will continue to grow more resilient. Each time you bounce back from a setback, you are strengthening your resiliency. Each time you accept a setback without attempting to come back, you are weakening that resiliency. If Weston had retreated from new challenges, for example, by giving up her career goals when she was fired, she would have returned spiritually to the passive, compliant girl she had once been.

We have said that we believe resiliency is learned and developed throughout a lifetime, from birth to death. Before we suggest the skills you need to learn to develop resiliency, we want to help you understand that "bouncing back" is not a leap upward from a trampoline but a three stage process.

The stages of resiliency

The stages are Holding on, Letting go, Moving on. You need to know what to hold, when to let go, and how to move on.

Holding On. You must learn not to hold on to the past when the past doesn't serve you well — or to a way of behaving because it has become familiar or comfortable — or even to a good idea when its time is over. Smoking is a familiar and comfortable habit, but no doctor today would suggest you hold on to that habit. Often people are afraid to let go of bad relationships or bad jobs. They stay in situations where they can no longer grow because they fear the unknown and cling to the "safety" of what is known. When challenged, they hold more tightly to that which gives them pain or stunts their growth because they are accustomed to that pain or they fear being hurt by change.

But there are some things you should hold on to tightly. Holding fast to your deepest beliefs in the face of a setback is the first requirement of resiliency.

"When I am down, I hold tightly to my faith in God," a friend told us. "I know that faith will see me through whatever happens in this life."

Your faith may be in God, family, friends, yourself, a commitment to which you have dedicated your life, such as teaching, health care, the ministry, even running a company that operates ethically in an unethical business environment. It may be a bedrock belief in the transcendence of human life. As you struggle with challenge, you must hold on to those core beliefs which define not only your life philosophy, but your life.

"How do I know if I'm holding on to my beliefs — or being selfish and refusing to accommodate others' wishes?" a woman asked us recently. "You have to get along with people in life. Sometimes that means giving in, doesn't it?"

Yes, you have to make both personal and professional compromises in life. Your partner wants to have dinner at a Chinese restaurant and you're in the mood for Italian. She gets a good job offer in another state, but you don't want to move. A co-worker doesn't like your proposal for handling a new account and thinks he has a better idea. Every day you are confronted with situations that require compromise.

Discriminating between core beliefs and transient desires is easier if you can identify and articulate those beliefs. Personal wishes — like the choice of a restaurant or even the city in which you live — can usually be compromised to accommodate others' wishes and needs without resulting in a loss of integrity. But know your bedrock beliefs and don't betray them for convenience or profit or the illusion of safety and security.

Clinging to some beliefs, however, can become the first barrier to the development of resiliency. Holding on to a good idea or a good value can keep you from bouncing back if you've held that idea or value too long, after it no longer serves you well. Most of us believe that loyalty, for example, is a good value. Should you remain loyal to the boss who was your mentor by remaining with the company after you've outgrown the job and there's no room for advancement? Or should you put your resume together, look for work that challenges you — while respecting and acknowledging the boss's contribution to your career?

Resiliency requires us to use our values as a springboard to growth. It teaches us not to empower ideas, but to use ideas to empower ourselves. Remember that resiliency is always grounded in reality and infused with hope.

If you're grappling with a challenge that causes you to confront your beliefs, ask these questions:

• Is this an idea or belief that really serves me well?

• Am I holding on to someone else's belief because I want that person's approval more than I want to develop my own beliefs?

• Is this a core belief — like faith in God — or a belief which should be periodically reexamined — like faith in a political party?

Letting Go. Some people know how to use the past to teach them about the future. They look into the past as if it were a crystal ball through which they can see the future. The lessons of the past stay with these people, while the extraneous details do not.

"When I hear forty-year-old men and women complaining about how their parents didn't give them enough love or support when they were children, I know I am lucky that I was able to let go of those feelings," said a friend whose own childhood was marked by parental neglect and verbal abuse. "Life is just too short to hang on to those grudges. I was careful not to repeat my parents' mistakes with my own children.

"But I forgave them for what they did to me a long time ago. If you hold on to your anger and resentment, you hurt yourself."

Letting go can be the hardest stage of resiliency. If you get rid of your past hurts, the ideas you've held for a lifetime, old work habits, and destructive attachments or relationships — what do you have left? You may feel like someone who has finally cleaned out the storage closets. Everything you didn't need or use is gone, but nothing is in its place. What do you do with all that space now? We have found that most people feel considerable anxiety during the pause between letting go and replacing the things left behind with new ideas and visions.

"Where do I go from here?" is the question we frequently hear from people in this stage of resiliency.

"What if I don't ever find someone I can love?" asked a man who had left an unsatisfying relationship.

"What if my money runs out before I find a new job?" asked a woman who had resigned rather than accept a demotion and cut in pay when her company was restructured. "What if I don't like my new job? What if I'm kidding myself in thinking that I have so much to offer? Maybe my mother was right when she said, 'You've made your bed, now you have to lie in it.'"

Sometimes people resist moving on at this stage. They choose to go back to the safety of the abusive boyfriend, the drugs, the bottle. Or they take a new job which is just like the old one because it was the first offer and they feared there would never be a second. Their desire to change or the determination to do so isn't strong enough.

"Nothing can ever change," a man told us, excusing himself for falling back into his old pattern of depression.

But resiliency tells us that things can and do change. During this pause — which can last a few weeks or much longer depending on the nature of the setback — you may have to fight the temptation to fill up your empty spaces, the spaces you have just cleared, by bringing back the same old ideas and habits and ways of behaving. This is a tricky period but you can learn to embrace it.

"Letting go left me empty for a while," said a woman who is working hard at learning resiliency. "But it was a good emptiness."

Moving on. If you don't turn back, the anxiety about change will eventually pass. One day you will realize that you are ready to embark upon a new path. You may wonder why you were so fearful.

"How could I have had so little confidence in myself?" marveled one man after he made his "mind leap" into the stage of moving on, the replacement phase.

The mind truly must leap over the pause — that anxiety-ridden empty space — into the new challenge. Many people tell us that once they have made their own leap, they look back across the chasm from the other side and marvel at the fear which held them in place for so long. The new, they report, feels "real" and "vital." Retreat never does.

An abrupt moving on

"Basically I am a coward, and all the things I'm not afraid of make me nervous," says teacher Penny Turk, a breast cancer survivor who suffered two mastectomies and six months of chemotherapy.

The "second most difficult period" of her life occurred in 1970-1971, her husband's tour of duty in Viet Nam. Left alone with two daughters, ages one and three, one of whom had medical problems, Turk was fearful of driving on the freeways, scared of balancing the checkbook, scared when the phone rang and "when things went bump in the night." She was nervous in strange bathrooms for fear she wouldn't be able to manipulate the door lock and would be trapped for hours. And, her mother's death two years before and her best friend's move across the country had left her feeling isolated.

She says, "I suppose I would have endured the year that way. Then at three o'clock one morning, a tremendous crash in the kitchen pulled me out of a peaceful sleep. I charged down the hall, yelling, 'Who is in here!' prepared to defend my children and my home from whatever intruders were there.

"I groped for the light switch. The kitchen, once illuminated, looked as it should with one exception. The spoon rack had fallen off the wall and attacked the table, sending a barrage of souvenir spoons exploding across the linoleum floor. No enemy at all! And yet I had vanquished my greatest foe.

"Once back in bed, I realized that I had thrown myself against the worst kind of imagined terror with no other thought than absolute fury that anyone would dare to violate the sanctuary of my home. I might be shaky on the exterior, but I had a core of indomitability which refused to be defeated.

"I'd like to tell you I was never frightened again, but there was the car trouble late one night alone with the children, during the big Los Angeles earthquake of 1971, and when the news reported that the ammunition dump one mile from my husband's compound had gone up with the explosive power of several atom bombs. That big war was still out there demanding to be felt, but in my own little war, I had won a major engagement."

Don't be discouraged if your own pauses take longer than you wish they would. As long as you haven't retreated to old patterns, old ideas, old behaviors, you've already begun to move on. Moving on, the final stage of resiliency, is the process of replacing what you left behind with what you hope for in the future.

PART TWO

RESILIENCY:

WORKING ON IT

CHAPTER FOUR

GETTING IT INTO PERSPECTIVE

"**S**hortly after the birth of my beautiful baby boy, I was diagnosed with leukemia," says Bethany Rossi. "At the same time, my husband was suffering business difficulties that were overwhelming him and threatening our financial security. Soon, he lost his business. We were both unemployed, dealing with a new baby, and facing a life-threatening disease — all with no income. All around us doors seemed to be closing.

"For a while it seemed impossible to change anything, even to hold on to each other. Relationships are terribly challenged when people must face extreme stress and strain each day. With the support of our families and friends, we did get past the despair and realized that we had the willingness, the desire to survive together.

"In that terrible time, we gained something we had lost. We gained perspective on life. We saw what was really worth holding on to, what we should let go of, what we loved in each other. We accepted that the bills would eventually get paid and trusted that the doctors would help. We became clear in what we wanted — to hold our marriage and our family together — and we focused on that.

"We learned that life does go on. You get through the pain and heartache. The pendulum does swing back — if you don't lose your perspective on life."

Bethany's leukemia is in remission. Her husband is working again and the bills are being paid. They know that her illness could come back, that new tragedies, financial or otherwise, could strike them. But they also know they will get through the bad times because they have each other, their families and friends. They know what is important in life for them: People and love.

What is perspective?

Perspective is your point of view on life. It is a coherent system of beliefs centered in one big idea which is close to the heart — like God, love, family, achievement, community, work — and infuses life with a sense of meaning. Without perspective, you begin to feel disoriented —

uncertain of what you want, who you are, or what really matters to you. People who keep their perspective filter everything through the prism of their core beliefs and are constantly grounded and comforted by them. No matter what happens to them, their faith in the importance and the truth of their deepest beliefs and values serves as their moral compass.

Resilient people have a positive point of view. Some people, as we've seen, develop that in childhood. Positive perspective is linked to the attribute of "coherence" in naturally resilient children. Resilient adults are possibility thinkers who refuse to fall into belief systems that support negativity, failure, and hopelessness. In fact, a positive perspective is an essential ingredient of resiliency.

"I don't like trouble any more than the next person," a friend said, "but I recognize that trouble always gives me the opportunity to make changes in a constructive way. More often than not, a problem causes me to examine my actions and see where I have strayed from who I really am and what I believe."

In other words, trouble gives this friend the opportunity to check his perspective.

The different faces of perspective

Faith. Bethany Rossi's faith is in the love of family and friends. For many people, it is God, in whatever way they choose to define God and worship.

Robert B. Pamplin Jr., author of *Heritage and Heroes*, speaks for many when he says that "faith is the cornerstone of resiliency." Without faith in something greater than ourselves, he believes, people cannot be strong enough to face serious challenges. The self is simply too insubstantial to carry the weight. Pamplin passionately believes that a person needs to adhere to basic ethical and moral standards as emphasized in the Judeo-Christian tradition to sustain resiliency.

There are many religious and spiritual belief systems in the world, each with its own devout and passionate proponents. Any deeply held belief system seems to support and protect resiliency in the people who embrace it.

An Indomitable Belief in Life. Some resilient people would not describe themselves as devoutly religious. They have instead an indomitable interest in life itself. To them, life is a gift. They can accept the many imperfections in this gift without judging it too harshly because they believe so strongly in the absolute value of life itself.

"I have long known that I could join the ranks of pessimists," says Robert Muller, assistant secretary general of the United Nations. "I can look at the war, the pestilence, the hunger — and let myself see little else. Or I can look at the distance we have come with many problems, in some areas, in stopping cholera, in zero population growth in some areas. I choose the latter perspective so I can go on living and working purposefully."

His is the resilient choice. Negative perspective limits resiliency, while a positive perspective supports it.

Love of Nature. Another perspective that sustains many people throughout their lives is love of nature. They report that simply observing the wonders of the natural world keeps their perspective in place.

"My husband and I moved to Montana," said Cathy Hastings, "because we had lost our perspective on what really matters while living in New York City and Los Angeles. We need to be surrounded by the outdoors, to live close to the land and the sky. Otherwise we let the petty concerns of daily life assume monumental importance.

"You can't take yourself and your little worries so seriously out here, surrounded by this vast and beautiful country. You know that your time on this earth is short and that most of the things which occupy you each day mean very little. Nature restores us. The cities never did."

Belief in Humankind Some people are resilient because an active urban life fills them with many possibilities and resources; others because they are thoroughly grounded in family or community traditions. Their faith in the transcendent goodness of those traditional beliefs sustains them.

In this country, immigrant families often have a strong tradition of valuing education. Parents frequently sacrifice a great deal to educate their children well.

"Nothing has ever been a threat to my survival," says Togo Tanaka, an eighty-year-old Japanese-American educational and cultural writer, who endured internment in a relocation camp during World War II, business failures, his cancer and his wife's cancer.

"My parents came to this country from Japan and worked hard to give their children an education," he says. "They believed strongly in education and the life of the mind. Our life was good until World War II."

Then, at 25 years old, Tanaka, a college graduate and pacifist who was writing for a Japanese newspaper in Los Angeles was arrested, along with thousands of other Japanese-American citizens on the West Coast, and sent to a relocation camp. He lost his job and his business before finally being rescued by the American Friends Service Committee and then moved to Chicago.

Tanaka's belief in education, pacifism, and "the life of the mind" which he learned from his parents gave him the resiliency to view that terrible period as "a challenge." His commitment to a scholarly lifestyle has sustained him through other setbacks. A magnetic man who plays an active, influential role in the community, he values intellectual curiosity over monetary gains or other comforts.

"I do not expect too much so my disappointments are not too great," he says. "I appreciate everything and never feel sorry for myself. I have never placed great reliance on material things. I see people giving too much meaning to things and then being devastated by the loss of them.

"I learned very early in life that material losses simply don't matter."

Pragmatism. Some people get their resiliency from their active engagement in problem solving. Action and results-oriented, pragmatists have a unique perspective: they see challenge as the very meaning of life. While many people take setbacks very personally and dwell on their feelings about it, pragmatists see the problem and look for the solution — without taking the situation very personally.

Sondra Lee, president of a private educational foundation, loves to solve problems. "When I was quite young, other children called on me to help them with everything from personal dilemmas to school work. My mother never overcame her shyness as a new immigrant to this country, so I negotiated everything for her outside of the home and advised her and my younger sisters and brothers as the eldest child. In high school, two of my teachers believed that my knowledge in their subjects almost surpassed their own so they allowed me to assist them in the classroom

"I entered university when I was fifteen and did very well. After college, I always began assisting, then advising, then mentoring my supervisors. I suppose you could say I was a born leader. I thrive on responsibility and finding solutions to problems — the tougher, the better!"

People may acquire at times a level of objectivity that is super-human, in order to handle superhuman challenges. In such cases even the most awful events provide them with material for problem solving, for strengthening their resiliency.

In *Man's Search For Meaning*, author Victor Frankl described how his mind "detached" when he was being stripped in a concentration camp.

"I was seized by curiosity," he reports. "I felt my mind become detached from its surroundings. I developed a kind of objectivity then."

Though he was held prisoner under barbaric circumstances, Frankl felt that his spirit was free because his mind was free. He could watch what was happening to him and other prisoners in a pragmatic way. No doubt this ability helped him face the challenges of each day as problems he could solve. His perspective on life gave him resiliency in a situation that would — and did — crush most people.

Higher Consciousness. The emphasis on individualism, self-esteem, self-awareness, and self-actualization which marked the closing decades of the twentieth century as being different from the eras preceding it has created a new perspective on life for some people: higher consciousness. This New Age perspective is more prevalent among those born during the 1960s and later. Some have integrated the concept of higher consciousness into more traditional belief systems.

"I would never have been able to cope with life's setbacks without the lessons I've learned from seminars on self-actualization," says Mary Howard. "I have learned to identify the behaviors that get in my way. When I was fired, for example, I retreated for a while. That was for me at the time a typical response to challenge — to get scared and hide. I would sleep until afternoon, get up, turn on the television, and eat a whole carton of ice cream. A friend dragged me to a seminar that changed my life because I discovered I had the power for positive change inside me."

After that seminar, Howard became a regular consumer of self-actualization programs. She says her self-esteem has increased as she has learned to handle setbacks by looking more deeply inside herself for the strengths and "healthy behaviors" that will help her bounce back. Yet Howard still describes herself as a "practicing Presbyterian." She attends church regularly and sees her newfound faith in herself as compatible with, not in opposition to, religious faith.

A strong perspective of positive self-development can be the source of resiliency for many people.

Why is perspective important?

Without perspective, you have to spend too much time thinking about what is important when life blindsides you. What you should hold on to? What you should throw away? What really matters? What do you stand for? Without perspective, you don't have the answers to those questions. How can you be resilient if you have to find the answers when you are in emotional turmoil?

When faced with a tremendous setback, people either give up or move on depending on how resilient they are. Any perspective can be challenged and threatened during personal tragedy. At such times, the resilient person reaches out for anything that is supportive until perspective is regained.

"I thought that if I was a good girl, nothing bad would happen to me," says Sandy Peckinpah, who discovered her own inner resiliency after her third child was born with a birth defect — the first truly serious personal setback of her life.

The eldest of five children, Peckinpah was the product of a solid, loving family, a responsible girl who made straight A's, didn't drink, "wasn't wild," went to church on Sundays, and sang with "Up With People," a musical touring group who promoted a "You Can Do It!" message, like the belief system she'd learned at home. Like her siblings, she made a strong marriage. Committed to the idea of "pulling together when trouble came," she formed a "phone tree" to provide information and support for family and friends and a prayer line for group prayer and meditation when her brother's baby was born with a heart defect. A source of support to her siblings, she and her husband, David, seemed to have the perfect life in Hollywood filled with friends, money, success.

"When I discovered my baby had been born with a cleft lip and gum," she says, "I threw my Bible across the room I was so furious. How could this be happening to me?"

Suddenly she'd learned that "good girls" sometimes had bad troubles. The period of anger was brief. She reached out to family, friends and a counselor for the help she needed to get through this "black hole." And she employed a mental imaging technique: she imagined happier times. Surgeries healed her child — and resiliency healed Peckinpah.

Unfortunately those were not her darkest days. Years later, she lost her first child, Garrett, at age sixteen to bacterial meningitis, an illness almost impossible to detect and treat. A doctor had diagnosed his illness as the flu.

"He was worse during the night," she says. "We called the doctor again, but he reassured us, on the assumption that Garrett had the flu. In the morning, when I went into his room, I started to scream. The paramedics came and they would not say if he was alive or dead. But I knew. I called a friend to stay with the children."

31

With her minister's help, she became the source of strength for David and her other three children after Garrett's death. Refusing pills to ease the pain, she focused her energies on caring for her family. And again, she imagined happier times.

"I reached back into the earlier years and imagined the family happy again," she says. "And I developed a program of healthy living so we would not compromise our lives with sickness. I developed traditions and rituals in the family that increased communication between us so we could share our experiences and our feelings.

"I liked my life before Garrett died, so I had to find a way to include death into my life. I developed a ritual of cleaning his gravestone, like I used to clean his room. I did this every day.

"I choose to believe my son is in heaven and that we will see each other again."

Without perspective, people who have suffered the loss of loved ones and other great tragedies may find it almost impossible to value life. Plunged into an abyss of feelings, the rudderless person becomes confused, disoriented and despairing. Perspective interrupts the downward spiral and helps us reconnect and commit to the world of the living.

How does perspective work?

You don't suddenly develop perspective in a crisis. You may have good ideas about how you want to live your life or how you want to cope with crisis. But having an idea doesn't mean you have perspective. You have to learn and develop perspective through study, dialogue and practice on a regular basis.

There are several ways to do that.

• *Meditate and pray regularly.* If your perspective is based in God, religion and spiritual faith, you need to practice that faith and pray on a regular basis. Reflect and meditate on your beliefs — and then apply them to your life. This systematic practice of faith helps develop and strengthen perspective.

- *Seriously challenge your mind.* Read good books. Listen to books on tape while you drive. Watch educational programs and participate in discussion groups, including church groups, professional groups, special interest groups and other groups centered around learning. Engage ideas and people and expand your perspective by learning how others meet challenge.

- *Develop relationships that encourage you to think.* When you suffer a setback and want to reach out to others for support, they won't be there for you in any meaningful way if you haven't cultivated the relationships. Close connections enrich your life through good times and bad, only if they permit real sharing and aren't limited to social "chat."

- *Get in touch with nature.* Take hikes, walks, strolls in the outdoors. Plan weekend day trips to nearby nature areas. If you live in a congested city, find that spot of green, even if it's only a pocket park. Plant a windowsill garden. Or go to a pond or an ocean. You will be able to think more clearly and calmly in the presence of nature because nature seems so timeless and resilient that our problems are made smaller in its presence.

- *Get interested in your work.* Put energy into problem solving at work — rather than nursing or repeatedly airing your same old grievances about the way the office is run. Share your ideas with your boss, colleagues, and professional group members. Have a positive attitude about change. And, look for ways you can make creative contributions even if they aren't part of your job description.

If you look at life through a small and narrow window, your perspective is no broader than the tiny window. By constantly striving for growth through learning and interacting with others, you continue to expand your perspective. If you do this regularly, you acquire new skills, ideas and viewpoints that become your own over time. After reading several books, for example, you learn to become a more critical reader. Listening to music develops your "ear" for music, or your ability to interpret and evaluate musical sounds and compositions.

Johnny Cash, the renowned country and western singer, has had a lot of troubles, many of them self-imposed in the early days of his success. He pulled himself out of trouble with rigorous discipline. "I pray daily," he told us. "I read scripture at least once a day and I study the Bible seriously. I also practice and develop my beliefs by writing them in song, including songs about trouble. By working on my talent, I also work on my faith. On bad days, I just pray more!"

Perspective can be expanded — broadened and deepened — so that it can help you find your way in the confusion following a crisis.

CHAPTER FIVE

AUTHENTICITY
AND
CONSCIENCE

As a child, Joel Block couldn't reconcile who he knew he was with how he was perceived by his teachers.

"Every week, tests were given," he says. "The students were seated for the rest of the week according to their grades. I vied with another boy for the most weeks in The Dummy Row at the back. I remember vividly when he spit across the room at the 100 percent papers posted on the wall. The teacher yelled at him. He threw a chair in her direction and walked out. He never came back, so I held the record for the longest stay in The Dummy Row."

By the age of eleven, Joel accepted his teachers' evaluation of him and believed that he was dumb. When he graduated from high school, he was rebellious and out-of-control. But he did have a "bull dog" determination and tenacity.

"If I found something I liked, like boxing, running, biking — I never let up. I was fiercely competitive to the point of self-injury at times, because I wouldn't give in to limits."

After a year of working at hopeless jobs after high school, he enrolled in night school. Deep inside himself, Joel believed he could do better. During the next year, he stopped seeing his friends, who were all settled in low-end jobs. Toward the end of the year, an admissions recruiter from a nearby college interviewed him. Joel made a good impression and got accepted at the state university, where he qualified for free tuition and loans.

By college graduation, he had discovered a natural aptitude for psychology. A psychology professor spotted his talent and ability, gave him his first "A" and the encouragement to continue in the field. He'd also learned to study and begun his relationship with his wife, someone committed to education. He began graduate school on probation, but beyond that point, Joel's story is one of determination and success. A straight-A student, he graduated at the top of his class, with a Ph.D. in psychology from an excellent university.

Almost fifty-two years old, Joel has been happily married for almost thirty years, has a son just graduating from college and a daughter working toward her Ph.D. A successful clinical psychologist, he is also the author of five books. Now he realizes that he suffered in childhood from a mild learning disorder which was not understood in his school.

How did he make that long journey from The Dummy Row to the head of the class? He gives a lot of credit to his mother, who though uneducated, was wise, observant, and supportive of him. He married an educated woman rather like her. Joel was able to parlay that early bonding experience into supportive attachments to others in his life. He is proactive and has a work-oriented, pragmatic perspective.

"I've always really believed the old adage that luck is 90 percent perspiration and 10 percent inspiration," he says. "I believe that the capacity to work hard is a gift for people who are willing to put out. I have an 'effort orientation' rather than an 'outcome orientation.' The only time I'm hard on myself is when I didn't try hard enough. If I tried, I feel okay about myself even if I'm disappointed in the outcome."

As an indomitable child, Joel was able to survive though he was forced for a time to accept his teachers' definition of him. As an adult, he resolved the split by coming to understand his earlier learning disorder and by persisting until his real self was expressed in every area of his life. He is a resilient and authentic person.

What is authenticity?

Authenticity is real, while inauthenticity is not. When we say an antique is "authentic," we mean it is the real thing — an 1820 pie safe, for example, and not a carefully distressed modern reproduction of an 1820 pie safe. Sometimes it takes an expert to authenticate antiques or works of art or valuable jewelry, because good fakes can fool the untrained eye. Inauthentic people fool most of us at least some of the time, too — but they never fool themselves.

When your behavior honestly reflects your inner thoughts and feelings, you feel authentic. If there is a serious split between how you behave and how you feel and think, you are living your life in a false personality. Real thoughts and feelings are suppressed. Gradually over time, the false personality becomes bigger. You tend to lose track of which parts were invented to please or impress which groups of people and become isolated within the intricate web of falsehoods and half-truths.

Unfortunately "faking it" is commonplace in this society, both on the public and private levels. Political and business leaders are almost expected to be dishonest. Ordinary citizens embroider their resumes and underestimate their taxes, exaggerate their attributes in singles ads, and lie about their marital status when they meet strangers out of town. There are people in the homosexual community who have never told their parents who they really are for fear of their parents' inability to ever accept them. And some people live in their false personalities twenty-four hours a day, hiding behind the polished images they consider more attractive than their real selves.

Are you real?

Charlie Estes, nicknamed "Charming Charlie," is a prominent theatrical agent, admired for his ability to remain unruffled and unfailingly courteous in his business and social dealings with clients, producers and others. His staff usually sees another Charlie, a man with an alarmingly short fuse. One day he chastised his secretary for bringing him a sandwich with mayonnaise, not mustard.

When she said, "But you told me..." he threw the sandwich against the wall and walked past her out of the room, muttering, "stupid..."

Who's the real Charlie? The nice guy or the tyrannical sandwich thrower? Are *you* living in a false personality or are *you* real?

A real person expresses real thoughts and feelings every day. Perhaps the genuine person inside Charlie's charming persona was ridiculed as a child. Maybe he was called names like "stupid." And maybe his anger at that past and at himself for living a false life sometimes erupts as it did the day his secretary forgot the mustard.

Charlie is an inauthentic person. He isn't real. Anyone close to him knows that he isn't, because his anger at the role playing is just below the surface of his charming persona.

How does inauthenticity develop?

Like most problems, it typically starts at home. Indomitable children with natural resiliency are less defensive and more open than other children. Their more authentic personalities elicit positive responses from others. Thus they form bonds that help them develop resiliency as they grow.

Many children are not encouraged to develop their real selves and are instead given many opportunities and resources to develop slick facades while their inner lives remain undeveloped. They learn what actions and behaviors win acceptance and praise from parents, peers, teachers, and others. Yet parents may actually spend little intimate time with these children, not asking them, for example, what they think and feel, or not teaching them how to heal their emotional wounds when they have been hurt.

As this child grows, he learns to hide his real self, shriveled and underdeveloped, behind a well-protected social facade. The slick real estate broker who wins sales awards, the CEO of a megacorporation, the honored Harvard Ph.D. — all may be inauthentic people afraid of being found out as frauds, ashamed of the thoughts and feelings they keep inside. Millions of people suffer from this split between the real self and the public self.

The writer, Christopher Lasch, was one of the first to describe this time in history as "the age of narcissism." The word "narcissist" makes us think of people in love with themselves — which isn't the case. Rather, they have fallen in love with a false personality, based on some idealized version of how they think they should be. But they don't like, love, or trust their real selves.

Why do you need authenticity?

You cannot develop resiliency if you are lying to yourself. The insecure person who hides inside a polished public face feels guilty for telling lies as well as guilty for not being a real person. Driven by a need to be safe, the result is a life based on adaptation and manufactured feelings, tastes and opinions. This is definitely not the way to develop real resiliency. How can you have a positive perspective on life if you're guilty all the time?

"You may be able to hide from people but, in your heart, you know who you really are," says Helena Beasley, who found the courage to be her real self in her early forties after her son angrily denounced her for repeatedly lying to him about her financial status, her accomplishments, her future plans.

She says, "I somehow got the message in childhood that I wasn't good enough. My mother was young and unmarried when I was born. In those days, pregnant girls were sent away somewhere to have their babies and put them up for adoption. She chose to keep me, but she paid a big price for that courageous choice and so did I. The man she married adopted me, but I was not the same to him as my half brother and sister, the children they had together."

Beasley started a lifelong pattern of lying when she was a child. She came home from school and told her mother and stepfather that she had made the highest grade on a paper when she hadn't or been chosen to play the lead in the school play when she'd really been assigned a minor role. Their praise for her false personality only reinforced her belief that her real self wasn't good enough. Lying became her way of dealing with the world until that emotional confrontation with her son which changed her life. And the lying had left her with a lifetime build-up of guilt.

"My conscience bothered me so often," she says. "I knew I was doing wrong by presenting myself as being better and smarter and more accomplished than I was. I never had a clear conscience until I started telling the truth."

If you are living a lie, your conscience really can't tell you what to do because you can't hear it clearly. That cacophony of sounds in your head produced by guilt — the inner voices shaming you for lying and not being good enough — makes your true conscience barely audible. The guilt that accompanies false personality also makes it hard for some people to change. Their "conscience" bothers them when they lie, but it bothers them more when they challenge the family belief system and try to change the childhood script written by their parents. "Change" would mean pursuing their own identity and discarding the facade known by family and friends. Like Beasley, they wouldn't have projected that false personality in the first place if they hadn't known it would be well received.

How can you become a real person?

It's easy to say, Stop being the false person and start being yourself! - but it's not always easy to do that. Let's take it in steps.

• *Challenge the attitudes, beliefs and feelings that support "no change."* Maybe you believe, "No one at this party will be interested in me if I say I'm a secretary so I'll say I'm a vice president instead." Examine that belief. Is it really true that secretaries aren't interesting? No. Is it really true that vice presidents are always interesting? No. Develop hobbies, take classes, learn, study, and read to become more interesting. Work to improve yourself. Don't fake it.

• *Act on the challenge.* As soon as you stop thinking about what you should do and start *doing* it, you have initiated change. You've broken an internal taboo that was keeping you in place. People who only think and don't act feel guilty because they haven't had the courage to act on their beliefs.

• *Kick the guilt habit.* Maybe you feel guilty about your real or imagined inadequacies — but feel just as guilty, or more so, about letting your real self emerge from behind the facade. In telling the truth, you may be betraying the belief system of your family. For example, there are women who tell their family that they are physically unable to conceive a child because they are afraid of the reaction to their decision not to have children. In families where abuse or addiction exists, lies hold the structure which supports the abuse or addiction in place. People pretend everything is all right. If you stop pretending, you may make everyone angry and also feel guilty about being separate. Your first responsibility is to develop your true self.

Reject learned guilt and push past your fears of being honest.

• *Expect to feel anxious.* You may be on the brink of saying "no" to guilt when suddenly anxiety kicks in. That anxious feeling is like a fever signaling that the body is in conflict. Examine the conflict. Is there a compromise between what you need to do to be true to yourself — and what others want or need from you? Don't let anxiety force you back into the guilt phase. Make the best choice you can for yourself and move on. Push through the fear that you, the real you, isn't good enough.

The good news about choices

When you make the right choices, you become authentic. We *are* our choices. Yes, it takes courage to overcome guilt, anxiety and fear and make the choice that is right for who we are, what we truly want, and what we really think and feel. You may fear that the consequences of a strong choice might be punishment, failure or success, commitment or separation, being found inadequate or being disliked.

"What if I push through the fear and make my best choice and find my best isn't good enough?" a woman asked us recently.

Sometimes our best doesn't win us the job or promotion, the love or admiration we crave. There are always a million reasons not to do the right thing. Fear that our best won't be "good enough" is one of them.

The power of choice is conscience

"My definition of resiliency is conscience, which is to be on the side of good," says Rabbi Harold Schulweis, the spiritual leader of Congregation Valley Beth Shalom in Encino, California. "Goodness is a remarkable spark. I went through a dark crisis of my own over thirty years ago. Facing my own mortality, I asked myself, 'If you come out of this alive, what do you want to do with your life?'

"I answered, 'Yes, I want to remain a rabbi and I want to be on the side of the good.'"

Rabbi Schulweis is an author, Jewish scholar, and the founder and chairman of the Jewish Foundation for Christian Rescuers, an organization that identifies and offers grants to those non-Jews who risked their lives to save Jews during World War II. His extraordinary commitment to a mission that bridges Jews and non-Jews is grounded in his belief that people should honor those who do good.

Rabbi Schulweis is concerned with the type of heroes we have today. People who make large amounts of money are revered. They include athletes and entertainers, high profile entrepreneurs, and some who are famous simply for being attached to the famous or for having been involved in a sensational scandal. The public seldom knows or even glimpses the real people behind the glamorous facades in this worship of style over substance.

"Our heroes today should be those people whose practice of faith led them to courageous actions," he says, citing the "righteous Christians" whose spiritual values transcended specific religious affiliation. "Their conscience told them to be on the side of good. We need to honor the unsung heroes whose acts of love are shining examples of the resiliency of ordinary people. We need models like Ann Frank's rescuers to show the rest of us how to increase resiliency. We confuse celebrity with heroism. You are not going to find heroism in the types exalted in the media."

Resiliency is the inner reward you receive when you heed the voice of conscience. At the moment when you choose to do the right thing - though it may not benefit you in any way — you have elected to be on the side of the good. And you hear, the Rabbi says,"the inner applause," congratulating you for doing the right thing.

"That is what makes one resilient," he says.

Often our ability to heed the voice of conscience depends on what we have learned from being knocked down in some way in our own lives. Hopefully, we've learned that a setback feels bad and we don't want to make others feel the same pain. We don't want to be the kind of person who knocks others down and justifies it by saying, "They'd do it to me if they had the chance." That person is mean spirited and merely tough — not resilient.

What is heroism?

When most of us read about people who have risked their lives to save others, we can't relate their stories to our own lives. We probably will never be faced with that kind of dramatic decision. For most people, heroism is the successful struggle to be real, to hear our conscience and be on the side of the good in the small life choices we make each day.

Maybe you don't feel particularly heroic or good, but you struggle constantly with issues of conscience. Will divorce hurt your children? If you are divorced, will they be hurt if you date or marry again? What will happen to a friendship if you date that friend's ex-boyfriend? Did you cause harm to someone by repeating gossip or engaging in office politics or by arbitrarily favoring one child or business partner or friend over another?

The difficulties most of us have with conscience are of the pedestrian kind — made more difficult because we are not always our authentic selves. Maybe you listened to the gossip with a pleasant expression because you feared expressing your true feelings and asking the gossiper to shut up. Or stayed in a stagnant relationship because you couldn't speak up for yourself.

One of the comments therapists often hear from super-achievers, successful executives, and professionals is: "I'm scared most of the time because I'm just faking. I'm afraid I'll be found out. Everyone will know I don't know what I'm doing then. I feel like a phony."

How can you stop feeling like a phony?

Some people think they will someday feel "real" if they achieve many successes, win awards, and have financial fortune, fame and acclaim heaped upon them. But they are wrong. Public acclaim or monetary fortune cannot bestow authenticity upon anyone.

Dr. Robert Pamplin Jr., who has had public acclaim, says, "The experience left me feeling humbled. Without character, the merit of any honorary plum shrivels like a prune. Without character, I never would have won anything, no matter what I was awarded."

Pamplin learned from his grandfather that "character is made up of integrity, trust and keeping your word." That lesson passed from one generation to another is part of his belief system. Commitment to this tenet requires consistency. Like Rabbi Schulweis, Pamplin believes that heroes and mentors can have great influence in our lives.

He says, "Counting on a man's word means you can count on his character — and character is a man's most important asset."

"Character" in this context is interchangeable with "authenticity." If you express real thoughts and feelings rather than the ones you believe will shore up the facade — you are authentic. Others can count on your word and your character.

The habit of authenticity

Resiliency in the face of setbacks requires the habit of authenticity. You can't be real in one situation and hide behind the facade in another situation without compromising that authenticity. We simplified the lessons of this chapter in the following checklist, which will help you stay real, in tune with your thoughts, feelings, and conscience — and able to bounce back from setbacks.

• Challenge your beliefs and behaviors that encourage inauthenticity.

• Kick the guilt that stops you from making choices for change and for good. Guilt keeps you involved in tortuous inner struggle — always questioning what is right and never having the confidence that you know the answer.

• Push through the anxiety and fear that accompany choosing change and that can paralyze you if unchecked.

• Check inside at important decisive moments to be sure your conscience is clear and your self-esteem is intact.

• Listen for the sincere inner applause that accompanies the choice for good.

• Proceed with confidence.

CHAPTER SIX

IMAGINATION
AND
HOPE

"**I** was my closest ally in childhood," says Bernadette Bowman, a struggling young actress who supports herself as an executive assistant between acting jobs. "My parents had screaming fights. My grandmother, who lived with us, basically wore the pants in the family and treated my father like the eldest child. I had two younger sisters and a brother. We all lived crowded together, an odd cast of characters all speaking very loudly. I couldn't bring friends home.

"But I always found great solace in my imagination and my spiritual side. I knew that was all I had. My heroines were television and movie stars. I wanted to be like Marcia on *The Brady Bunch,* because she was the girl my Granny — and the boys at school! — would have liked me to be.

"My role models were Susan B. Anthony, because we shared the same birth date, and Louisa May Alcott, because I loved and admired her talent as a writer. Books were a big escape for me.

"I knew, even at a very young age, that women were always getting the short end of the proverbial stick. As a first grader, I asked a visiting speaker from NASA, 'When are you planning to send a WOMAN to the moon?'

"My mother had to work, because my Dad's teaching salary was not enough. I just assumed that I would never be one of those women who watched soaps and ate bon-bons. I knew that I would be the one responsible for making my dreams come true.

"I was lucky to have a wonderful teacher in fourth grade who helped me develop confidence in myself. I wanted to be just like her when I grew up. She was a palette of so many wonderful colors, so bright and fresh, and not an unoriginal bone in her body. "And I was lucky to discover acting. Any audience gives me all the confidence I need."

Bowman's resiliency is rooted in hope — and her ability to imagine that what is not yet seen can be better than what is known.

What is hope?

Hope is the belief that the future you imagine can become a

reality. Without hope, we cannot imagine a future for ourselves. Hope is the voice of your authentic self. It expresses your dreams and aspirations, your deepest feelings and needs.

In his book *Images of Hope: Imagination As Healer Of The Hopeless*, William F. Lynch defines hope as the "fundamental knowledge and feeling that there is a way out of difficulty, that things can work out, that we ... can somehow handle and manage internal and external reality, that there are solutions..."

Long interested in the dramatic imagination, Lynch was inspired thirty years ago to write this classic book on hope by Dr. Karl Menninger who believed that patients who had a sense of hope had a better prognosis for recovery — all other things being equal — than those who felt hopeless about their conditions. As he began talking to people about hope, Lynch discovered that there was a "close bond" between hope and the life of the imagination.

In the first chapter, he wrote: "Hope involves three basic ideas that could not be simpler: what I hope for I do not yet have or see; it may be difficult; but I *can* have it— it is possible."

Hope is a sense of the possible which transcends the present moment. A cancer patient undergoing chemotherapy needs hope to envision that time when the cancer will be gone, the side effects of chemotherapy will be an unpleasant memory, and life will be good again. A talented and ambitious young person embarking on a creative career in a big city also needs hope to see a future bigger than a dark studio apartment barely big enough for a bed and chair.

The elements of hope

There is a link between hope and the "bonding" which is seen as an attribute in many resilient children. As children, their hope may have sprung from relationships that supported and encouraged them. It may also have developed spontaneously from the vivid imagination that is so much a part of childhood, and is characteristic of some children more than others. As adults, resilient people can also form those bonds with God or absent or invisible people, as well as real people in their lives. A writer, for example, imagines an invisible audience as he or she writes. In prayer, we talk to a God whom we cannot see.

Hopefulness is a trait of resilient people. And in them, hope has three critical elements:

- *Wider perspective.* When you imagine what you have not yet seen, you widen your perspective on life. "Hope imagines — and refuses to stop imagining," Lynch says. Rooted in realism, hope imagines the way out of difficulty.

- *Mutuality or collaboration.* "Hope not only imagines, it imagines *with*," Lynch says. Hope is tied to our relationships. If no one affirms your beliefs, values, feelings — you may become apathetic. Without affirmation, you may mistrust yourself. We all need supportive and responsive relationships to encourage our hope and help prevent us from withdrawing into hopelessness. People develop hope in each other.

- *Imagination.* Hope is wishing for a better future - and wishing is an important part of human life. When we can no longer wish, we are in despair. In fact, *apathy is the complete absence of wishing*. You must be in touch with your feelings, yearnings and values to know what you want — and for what you wish. And then you must attach scenarios you can "see" to your wishes. Daydream in complete sentences. Put yourself into your daydreams, so they become more real to you. Then your imagination will help move your wish to a practiced experience, and your wishes will feel more possible. Your imagination will even help you figure out how to make your wishes come true.

A portrait of hope

"My father taught us that, in times of trouble, you must look to the future and have hope," says Annette Albert, who is almost ninety years old. "He always said, 'Look to the mountain! And always remember that this too shall pass.'"

The fourth of seven children, Albert was born and raised in Cleveland, Ohio, in a deeply spiritual family. A teacher, scholar and philosopher — her father taught his children spirituality on a daily basis. She remembers him as a "gentle, quiet, serious man of enormous integrity and intellect, who spoke several languages and guided his family until the end of his life." His spirituality was based on hope — a strong belief in the future — and generosity.

"Spirituality was served with the cereal in the morning and the chicken in the evening," she says, laughing. "It was part of our daily diet."

Albert's mother supported those beliefs and values and reinforced them on the practical level through her personal habits and the traditions she developed for her children.

"The blue can taught us children the value of charity," she says. "My mother kept a blue can on the kitchen table. Everyone, from my parents to the littlest child, put a portion of their money regularly into the blue can. This money was donated to charitable organizations or needy individuals. Mother was a brilliant, cultured, dynamic woman who was ahead of her time in her commitment to philanthropy — and in her career. She had her own thriving real estate business."

Albert took the tradition of the blue can into her own marriage. Though she had to operate her household on a tighter budget than her mother had, she still supported charitable organizations throughout her life. In addition to the blue can, she had a second can — called "the maybe can" or "the nest egg" on the kitchen table when her own three children were growing up. The second can covered special needs or wishes or "treats."

"The maybe can paid for our wishes," she says. "Every time we put money in it, we wished for something. Maybe we could take a vacation. Maybe one of the girls could have a perm or a new prom dress."

This habit of hope, as exemplified by the savings cans, enabled Annette Albert to remain a resilient person through the losses of her parents, two brothers, two sisters, her husband, her only son, and many good friends.

"I believe that a resilient person has faith which fortifies the spirit to keep going for a better day," she says. Having hope, she believes, is like "putting deposits in your inner bank, from which you can draw when you are challenged or experience loss.

"I have never lost sight of my father's simple concept: 'Life goes forward, not backward; and there is no road that has no turning. You must have patience and faith and hope that everything resolves itself in time.'"

People without hope are emotionally and spiritually bankrupt because they do not believe in the future. They have no resiliency — no way to bounce back from the setbacks. Annette Albert's advice to them: "Do something! Do anything!"

The faces of hopelessness

The negative consequences of hopelessness are depression, apathy, and the death of the imagination or "wishing."

• *Depression.* People who are depressed don't have the energy needed for commitment to life, change, adaptation. They may feel as if some large weight were holding them down.

• *Apathy.* The apathetic often describe themselves as "bored." Nothing excites or interests them.

• *The death of the imagination.* Without hope, there is no wishing. People may substitute alcohol, food, antidepressants, illegal drugs, gambling, binge shopping or compulsive television viewing for their "wish list." The imagination has been stilled.

Some people who have experienced hopelessness in their lives compare it to being in a black hole.

"I remember reaching my darkest moment," says Jody Gillis, who suffers from degenerative arthritis in both knees, a painful condition which left her dependent on crutches and sometimes an electric wheelchair to get around.

"It took seven years of slow, gradual disability to arrive at the bottom of the black hole. But when it all began, I had no sense of what was coming. It started one evening in my home while my husband and

I played bridge with two good friends. Luckily, one friend was also our family doctor, for when I tried to get up at the end of the evening, my legs would not work. In great pain, I was helped to my bed. I remained on medication for some time. At one point, I was taken for X-rays which led to the diagnosis of degenerative arthritis.

"For one year, I functioned with one cane. During year two, I continued to work and function with two elbow crutches. For the next seven years, I taught elementary school in a wheelchair. I experienced surprise each time my condition grew worse, thinking 'Well, okay, so I need a cane — a crutch — not so bad.' I grew interested in problem solving as I watched my condition deteriorate. But when the pain of walking became so bad that I needed a wheelchair, the shades of gray I'd been seeing began to look a little black.

"By the time I reached the bottom of the black hole, I had been teaching from a sofa in the classroom for two years, but I was still handling it. Then the light went out. "I could see my depression getting deeper. It started as a field of pale gray surrounding me. The color deepened. I could see it deepen and was somewhat surprised that I could. Eventually the field of color became the deepest black. That happened when I could barely walk from the bed to the bathroom, which was only about ten steps. In the morning I would stand for a long time waiting to be able to move. Even my humor, which always saved me in any situation, began to fade. I was now in my early fifties and had been told no operation was possible until I was 65."

In her depression, Gillis could see nothing but pain and a downward spiral of physical deterioration. She had lost hope. Her story doesn't end in a black hole — as you will soon read — but sadly many stories do end there.

A depressed person has lost his ability to imagine a way out. The deeper the depression, the more the person believes in the hopelessness of his situation, whatever it may be. At some point, he can no longer enjoy life's pleasures, a good meal or a good book, sexual intimacy, contact with nature, a stimulating evening with friends, or playing with the children. Depression sounds like a passive state, but it is really an active, aggressive denial of pleasure and possibility, a denial that stops the person from change and growth, from moving on to the next stage in life.

Depression is also a hiding place, the place where one hides consciously or subconsciously from the challenges of life and from change. One person we know described that hiding place as an interior "sigh." But something as simple as hope can stop the sighing.

Another face of hopelessness

Depression and apathy are familiar enough images to most of us. You know what they look like because you have seen them, if not in your own mirror, then in the faces of others.

Another face of hopelessness is less easily recognizable because it masquerades as hope. Vacant hope is a condition of empty yearning, of unrealistic anticipation, or of frenetic activity that is going nowhere. Dr. Warschaw first described this subtle self-sabotage in *Rich Is Better*. Vacant hope is a way station on the continuum of hope to hopelessness. It is merely waiting for "something to come along" through activities that are disconnected from accomplishments or results.

With vacant hope, people may have a lot of starts, but few completions. Mixed signals are sent. Too much time is spent in preparatory detail. The man who lives in vacant hope flits from one half-finished project to the next, getting caught up in beginnings and middles. He may not necessarily be effective in a crisis, but he is excited by its element of novelty and relieved at the reprieve it seems to offer.

The woman who is involved in a long affair with a chronically promiscuous man whom she believes she will change lives in vacant hope. So does the woman going into business for herself with no knowledge of how to manage money. The unhappy wife in a barren marriage, the artist who has worked in a low-level "temporary" job for twenty years waiting for someone to notice his talent, the graduate student who hasn't earned a degree after years of study — all live in vacant hope.

Real hope is solid, with content as well as form. It is grounded in reality, not fantasy. Real hope is a wish with possibility. And real hope is what lifted Jody Gillis out of that black depression.

From despair to hope

Jody's husband was in an accident sometime after she'd been diagnosed with degenerative arthritis. His injuries required surgery.

"I never felt so alone or terrified," she says of his recovery period. "I didn't let my husband know how badly I felt. When I was alone, I would scream under a pillow and cry.

"His philosophy about life has always been, 'It's the only game in town, so play it.' My philosophy had always been, 'Don't feel sorry for yourself.' If I could stand in the middle of a street and ask people who have it worse than I do to step forward, I would be crushed in the stampede.

"These two life philosophies became my main resources during that difficult time. I kept repeating them to myself and eventually the black began to lighten again. At first I would only see a little pinpoint of light, but that encouraged me to say, 'Get on with it.'"

During her years in the wheelchair, she had been told by various doctors that she was too young for knee replacement surgeries. Due to limitations in the prosthesis available at the time, doctors preferred to operate on patients 65 or older. Then one day she saw a Phoenix doctor on a television talk show discussing his success with knee surgery and renewed her search for a local expert. She made an appointment with Dr. Michael Rodi of San Diego and had the operations, each requiring eight months of painful therapy afterward. "When Dr. Rodi warned me about the absolute necessity of therapy, my reply was 'Hey, I went to Catholic school; just tell me what to do and I do it!'"

"I had such faith and hope in my doctor," she says, "and that helped see me through. My husband Larry and my mother Ann were there for me, too, every step of the way. Larry had to help manipulate my legs and knees at least four times a day. My mom, who is usually one tough lady, would run to her room and hide when the moaning and yelling started. But the wheelchair was sold months ago and it was all worth it."

How you can develop hope and imagination

Do you want to be more hopeful? Then let's begin to work on imagination. "Imagining a way out" after a setback is the first step toward hope but it's also the hardest step to take. Imagination isn't the same thing as decision-making. It looks the same on the surface, but decision-making is pragmatic — it's "in the world" — and comes after you know where you want to go.

Imagination is related to vision; without yet deciding on the concrete steps to achieve it, you first need a "broad sense" of the ultimate destination. As Stephen Covey says in his book, *Seven Habits of Highly Effective People*, one of the maxims of effectiveness is to "begin with the end in mind." That's what is meant by vision. And in order to "envision it," you use the faculty called imagination.

A limitation of imagination has to be remembered, though. Remember that hope must be realistic to be real hope. This doesn't mean that you should talk yourself out of everything you might hope for by being so "practical" your imagination never has a chance to begin.

In fact the people who have the least imagination are often those whose parents discouraged every childhood hope and dream with "Who in the hell do you think you are?" or "Get real! Unlike your cousin Mary, you have no talent!" However, in order to bring imagination and dreams into reality, they must be based on some real ability or possibility. If you can't carry a tune and are tone-deaf, aspirations to be a singer because you love Barbra Streisand or Michael Jackson may not be realistic. Such fantasies are not hope, they are vacant hope that can only serve to prevent your arriving at achievable, possible goals — if you take it a step at a time.

Even so, you say, many geniuses flunked out of high school because they were bored, or like Joel Block, they sat in the "dummy row" and went on to Ph.Ds. It's true, there are always enough exceptions to any rule. Simply remember, you may be the exception to the rule, but try to ground your fantasies and dreams in some sense of reality. Joel had a real talent for psychology, which he discovered in college. What are your real passions, your real abilities, your real preferences? What are your resources and your chances?

If your assessment is that you can do it, then go for it. Pull in all the favors and supportive friends you've got to help you beat the averages. Regardless, doing something and wanting something very much will get you more than doing nothing at all. Making a little money is better than no money at all. Being a little fish in a big pond is much more than not wanting to swim at all. These assumptions are at the heart of hope. Hope that life has a place for you keeps you trying and wishing.

If you want to develop your imagination, we suggest that you try some of the techniques below. Make one or more of them part of your daily or weekly routine.

1. Pray or meditate regularly, whichever approach works best for you. The best time for these practices is just before sleeping or just upon awakening, when the conscious mind is least in control and you are closer to the unconscious or subconscious mind.

2. Pay attention to your daydreams, and take them seriously. Daydreams are influenced by our conscious mind to a degree that nightdreams are not, but a lot of the imagery in daydreams comes from exactly the same source as nightdreams. Both are rich sources of unconscious, creative, feeling-filled, personally symbolic ideas about our place in the universe, and both can be tapped in the act of imagining.

3. Join or start a small group of people committed to working on imagination and visioning. Most self-help groups still focus on problem solving and emotional support. Fewer work on creative imagination. We have run seminars to develop creativity. If you can't find any resource in your community, start a group with friends and

use this book and other handbooks on imagery to guide you through helpful exercises together.

4. Interpret your dreams and search for ideas in them about what you really want next. Talking the dream out loud often leads to an intuitive discovery of what it means; the dreamer needs to "hear it" to recognize the meaning in the symbols. Talk to a friend or a professional, who specializes in dream interpretations.

5. Read a book every month on imagination, imagery, dreams or inspirational topics. If you belong to a prayer group or a book discussion group, discuss the material with an eye to applying it to your own life. Biographies of people you admire are rich sources of hope and imagination. The bible is a book about people with personal stories, tales of courage, mistakes and redemption.

6. Look for models of your hope and imagination, those who are really living it. They are most likely positive thinkers. Avoid negative thinkers and dream-stealers, they can stop your imagination.

7. Practice imagining yourself mastering the things that frighten you. If you are in an abusive relationship you might see yourself in a new apartment, safe and content, surrounded by the things you love and people who support your well-being.

If you're afraid of confrontation, imagine yourself hanging on in a fight and holding your own or winning. If you are afraid to be alone, imagine yourself alone at night and calmly learning to enjoy and use the time. All people are basically fearful; those who you see as fearless are those who were trained from a young age to think positively about life. Even so, millions of people whose heads were filled with warnings and dire consequences by overanxious parents, teachers and not-very-good-friends, have learned to overcome their fearful fantasies and replaces them with affirmations. It works.

8. Talk to someone supportive about your hopes, fears and aspirations. If no one in your life believes in you, get out and search for people who will. Keep searching for a resource who understands your dream, takes it seriously and knows how to encourage you in bringing it down to earth. Joining traditional support groups, 12-step pro-

grams or self-assertiveness groups can be helpful as well as seeing a counselor, minister, rabbi, friend, teacher, coach or mentor.

You will find it difficult to hope without supportive relationships. That doesn't mean single adults are doomed to hopelessness. The caring relationship can be with family or friends, too.

In the absence of a mate, family, or friends, many people turn to professional helpers. Ministers, priests, rabbis, counselors or therapists can help you overcome problems that may have made you unable to form relationships. In psychotherapy, a client forms a deep, supportive bond with the therapist, a therapeutic relationship where his hidden wishes, guilts and fears can be brought into the open and healing can begin.

Once you have successfully expressed your true feelings and found healing in that experience, you will be able to do it more easily the next time. You can transfer the habit learned in therapy or in a support group to interacting with spouse, family, friends. As you share your thoughts, feelings, fears, desires — and wishes — you will begin to have real hope for the future.

Resiliency is most available to handle hopeless, irrevocable losses if you have years of practice in proactive problem management, collaborative relationships, and can-do attitudes.

Carole Hyatt, a high-powered entrepreneur, author and international public speaker, is also a wife and mother. By most standards, she has "the perfect life," with an enviable network of influential friends, family and career.

Now for the first time in her life, Carol has a problem she cannot solve or resolve. Her mother has Alzheimer's disease. Her mother had the kind of charisma that continued to attract interesting men at 75! Even now in her nursing home, she has a 90-year-old boyfriend.

"I'm sorry to tell you that your mother has Alzheimer's," she was told. Carol felt that the word alone was frightening. It reeked of the irreversible, abandonment and despair. "I felt mom had left me!" says Carol.

But Carol is drawing on many of the same sources of resiliency in this situation as she always has. She has immersed herself in all of the available research and calls on her international network to pursue the best drugs and to get the best help possible. She says, "When I am in action I know I am okay; if I lose control and there is nothing I can do I feel terrible."

CHAPTER SEVEN

NEGOTIATING
AND
COLLABORATION

"**M**y most successful experiences in resolving complex issues have always been when I was a leader of an extremely competent team," says Dr. Richard Varnes, an educator, psychotherapist, and organizational consultant with advanced degrees in engineering and clinical psychology.

"The teams can never be assembled again," he says. "But the unique experiences can be emulated." Dr. Varnes believes that "a continuous flow of excellent ideas" is "essential" for success in groups. While he does not discount the importance of good management methods and skills, he thinks that organizational success is dependent on negotiation and collaboration. A man who kept his resiliency through both personal and financial setbacks and a career change at age forty from nuclear engineering to psychology, Varnes credits his work with his ability to bounce back. Only someone who works the way he does would find that such a rich resource.

"Work as an external resource has without a doubt been my salvation," he says. "If I had to deal with the reversals that I have had in my life without work, I would be a basket case. Work is the place where possibilities of survival become obvious. At work, I feel the support of the community and use that energy as a spring-board to growth. "Ultimately," he says, "success has to do with the ability to adapt to a changing environment. This adaptation requires an occasional total renewal of the organization. 'Starting with a clean sheet of paper,' as they say."

Part of the renewal process — for companies as well as for people like Varnes — involves negotiation and collaboration. Work is a resource for resiliency when people have negotiating and collaborating skills. If they don't, work is often the breeding ground for burnout.

One of the most difficult career situations Varnes confronted occurred during his eighteen years with a major aerospace corporation, when he was working on a nuclear reactor project. While the engineering personnel assigned to the task were highly qualified experts, they were not performing as an outstanding group. Acting as project director, Varnes was able to get the engineers to work together on a complex design which he later presented at a plenary session of the American Nuclear Society.

His method? "Continuous exploration of the issues to be resolved," he says. Each member of the team had input into the exploration process. "It is difficult to describe the feelings and comradery that I enjoyed in this environment," he says.

An authoritarian manager would have dictated terms to his subordinates. By working through negotiation and collaboration, Varnes was able to help a group of brilliant people become more than the sum of their parts and he — and they — became more resilient.

What is negotiation?

Negotiation is simply the give-and-take process through which two or more people seek agreement. It isn't limited to business deals. Dr. Warschaw decided to write her best-selling book, *Winning By Negotiation,* because so many of the clients who consulted her about their personal problems responded with a blank stare or puzzled frown when she asked them: "Did it ever occur to you to negotiate?"

Many of those people had vast experience as negotiators in the business world. Yet they had no idea that the problems of everyday life could be solved through the techniques of business negotiation, too. By learning how to negotiate for power, for money, and for love and respect, with family and friends, and with professional and service people, some of them became so adept at getting what they wanted without taking anything away from others that Warschaw labeled them "Win-Win Negotiators." Resiliency, they have learned, depends on other people. When they attempt to solve any problem, the first question they ask is, "How will this affect the other person?"

Below is a four-step process that can help you organize your thinking in problem solving.

Four steps to a win-win

- *Define the problem*. When you look at a problem, you tend to see it from your own perspective, which is natural but not comprehensive. Until you've managed to see the problem from the other person's perspective as well, you haven't defined it.

- **Decide what you want.** Many people don't know what they want. First, determine what you *don't* want. Then, put aside your fear and figure out what you do want. Many people are afraid of the consequences of their desires and rarely admit they want something.

- **Design a strategy.** A strategy is a series of steps designed to achieve your objective. You know what you want. Now what is the logical plan of action? No strategy succeeds unless it springs from self esteem — that positive sense of self-worth that energizes us to act and to persist in goal-directed behavior. The two key elements to a successful strategy are timing and style, both your own and others.

- **Do It!** You've come a long way to get to this point. Your decision to act has been carefully considered. You've chosen your goals, examined your options, and devised your strategy. The time has come to act. Create a timeline to accomplish your goals. Trust yourself. We are committed to a philosophy of negotiation based on empathy and collaboration — an approach to problem solving that we believe supports resiliency. People who repeatedly and aggressively defend their positions or convictions become alienated from the group. Often they suffer from burnout. But those who take the group into consideration have the support they need to execute a plan. These negotiators are resilient people who recognize that they are living in the age of collaboration.

What is collaboration?

We believe that life as we enter the twenty-first century will be defined and driven by collaboration. What does that really mean? To us, it is quite simple: *Negotiation with affiliation.* A group has the power to augment and support and complement the individual. Whether that group is a family, social or work unit, it can empower the individual in a successful collaboration. Each member of the group grows more resilient.

Why is collaboration so essential now?

Tom Peters in his book, *Crazy Times Call For Crazy Organizations,* quotes David Vice, of Northern Telecom, "There'll only be two kinds of managers in the future... the quick and the dead." The quick have learned to collaborate. The dead tried to do it alone and collapsed from the effort.

Collaborative negotiators have a taste for change and believe there may be many possible solutions to any problem, many ways to respond in any situation. And, they are empathetic people who want a balanced life, the kind achieved only in community with others who also believe that caring and nurturing are reciprocal.

More people than ever are beginning to see the merit in a collaborative way of life. Some organizations now expect this style of negotiating from their managers, so that all sides walk away with something. That is a pragmatic, not a charitable point of view, because in the long run personal and company resiliency will depend more and more on collaboration.

The individual can't possibly learn everything he needs to know as quickly as he needs to know it — or master every necessary skill in an age when new technology mandates new skills at a dizzying pace. The Age of Collaboration is too technical, too complex, too fast, and too big for one person working alone. For the individual to succeed in the global economy where databases store massive amounts of information, he or she must be able to function with affiliation through teamwork.

Individuals who cannot work this way are susceptible to complete burnout, health problems, stress overload, disorientation, and serious family dysfunction. Look at the burnout syndrome in air traffic controllers, for example. They work under intense pressure and in isolation - and suffer from those conditions.

In her work with corporate leaders and senior executives, Dr. Barlow has heard a new fear expressed with growing frequency since 1990. Several women have told her they identify with an image taken from the film, *The Red Shoes.* They envision themselves dancing faster and faster, becoming exhausted, but unable to stop.

This image, Dr. Barlow believes, expresses the women's fear of manic hyperperformance which they can't control or stop. They are describing fear of burnout, a loss of resiliency, caused by their compulsive striving for perfection in careers that set no limits on how much it takes to succeed. Although men express it somewhat differently, they suffer from the problem as well. The need to control and the fear of spinning out of control — lead to burnout.

Exhaustion results in missing important cues about your situation until it's too late to regroup. Ken Michelson, for example, was a high powered executive until he was fired in a corporate downsizing.

"I did not see the firing coming," he says. "I was so tired from putting in eighteen-hour days that I misread the clues. None of my strategies were on target. I did not strategize my leaving."

Initially he was shattered by the firing, but later Ken saw it as a "blessing, an opportunity to regroup. "

A portrait of collaboration

"As a new manager, I tried to do everything alone," says Joanna Russo, a bank manager for a major metropolitan bank. "I thought my superiors would think I was stupid if I asked for support or help."

At the time Joanna was both a new manager in a new location and part of the merger of her bank with another bank. In moving to the location, she had essentially lost her "work family" from her prior position. Fifty years old and single, she was a self-described "loner" whose life revolved around work.

"The bank gave me no training for the new position," she says. "I was thrown into the midst of their corporate reinvention through acquisition with no support system. I felt set up for failure. Management gave us high goals, then told us we wouldn't make those goals. 'We expect people to fail,' they said.

"That attitude made me angry. The people who were making the decisions weren't walking the floor. Nobody listened to me. I felt like I was always running after the cart, with no hope of catching up."

She was under so much stress that she began to lose confidence in herself. Unable to negotiate anything with anyone, she assumed greater and greater responsibility at the office. On weekends, she slept. For a while, Joanna "sat on the mat," unable to bounce back from the setbacks. The turning point came for her when, at the encouragement of her therapist, she teamed up with another woman.

"I was determined not to fail, so I tried the buddy system," she says. "I got the support and help I needed from another manager with more experience and a more low-key style than my own — which is demanding, without being tough. We depended on each other not to stab the other in the back."

Through collaboration, Joanna cultivated her own strengths, which include a good sense of humor. She and her "buddy" were able to focus on the big picture when they no longer had to put all of their energy into dealing with crises, one after another. They also vented their anger at the demands the acquisition had placed on them by complaining to each other about district management. In being able to share their frustration with a trusted partner, they diffused much of the anger.

"Once I knew I wasn't alone, I could make specific goals," Joanna says. "I learned how to choose my battles. On the personal level, I forced myself to stop sleeping all day on weekends and vegging out in front of the TV when I wasn't sleeping. I began to exercise. I saw activity as a ladder which would get me out of the hole I was in." Joanna used three tools to build her resiliency.

• *Determination and belief in self.* Even though both were shaky initially, she shored them up.

• *The use of a buddy system.* Without the successful collaboration, Joanna was headed for burnout.

• *Moving the body.* She forced herself to stop sleeping so much and watching large amounts of TV and pushed her body into exercise.

Why is collaboration so important?

We believe that collaboration is the single most important skill to learn if you are going to adapt and survive in the new era. And it is necessary to sustain resiliency without paralyzing isolation or burnout. The need for collaboration goes beyond the traditional workplace.

Many families are now faced with the need to collaborate in the care of elderly parents. Unlike members of generations past, they may live in different parts of the country and have young families of their own and demanding careers. When everyone lived within minutes of each other and had several children at a young age and few wives worked, the care of elderly parents was relatively simple compared to what it is today. Even inside the nuclear family, collaboration is necessary if the daily chores are to be done in a home where everyone works or goes to school. How much more complicated life becomes for everyone in a medical or other emergency!

"My mother and grandmother were both diagnosed with the same degenerative disease," says Donna Alvarez, in her early thirties. "My grandmother had to be placed in a nursing home at the same time my mother was diagnosed and deteriorating rapidly. My older brother was trying to manage caring for both of them all alone. I was feeling torn apart until I arranged a long-term stay in my home town to help.

"I arrived with my new baby in tow. In spite of the fact that my brother and I had rarely spoken to each other in three years, I felt compelled to be there to help when the crisis hit."

Small business owners and entrepreneurs are also finding collaboration the answer to their problems. Increasingly, they are realizing they can't make it alone in today's competitive economy. Some consultants are forming consortiums for sharing referrals, achieving cost effectiveness through group buying, and emotional and more tangible means of support. And sometimes they have to rejoin the corporate world on a part time or other basis.

"I had a small but elite client base," says Richard Dugan, a consultant. "But over six years, the clients I'd brought with me from my corporate job had dwindled. I was depressed and isolated. Finally I sought counseling for that. I didn't know what to do. The counselor suggested that I build a new corporate base by going back to work for a corporation again.

"I did that for three years. When I left the corporate world again, I was energized and I had a new partner and a new client base. Group practice is working much better for me."

Perhaps nowhere is the importance of collaboration more evident than in the stories of people who paid a big price because they couldn't work successfully with others.

"I thought I could get away with anything at work because my job was 'safe,' " says Melanie Grayer. "I knew that I was very good at what I did. I tolerated no feedback, no opposition. If people did challenge my ideas, I furiously assaulted them. I thought I had unwritten permission to treat others sarcastically because I was so good — and I thought that right up until the day I got fired for being a 'disruptive and destructive force within the company.'

"I still didn't get the message, but I decided to become an entrepreneur. When I realized I needed cash and clients, I learned to sweeten up my act. I'm still tough, but I have learned how to negotiate and collaborate with people. I've learned that I need people not just for cash but for brainstorming ideas, for support."

Melanie was always a tough negotiator who knew how to win for herself, but she learned to be a collaborator, which has allowed her to be more resilient. A philosophy that does not encourage people to support you also does not give you a chance to build your own resiliency. When you become harsh, shrill, dictatorial — you also become rigid and less resilient.

The elements of negotiation and collaboration

Negotiation and collaboration in adults is related to the proactive style and adaptability observed in naturally resilient children.

Remember, those children engage in problem solving at an early age. When confronted with obstacles, they meet, rather than withdraw from, the challenge.

Jason Houghton, a little boy who was verbally and occasionally physically abused by his father survived with his resiliency intact because he knew how to find a safe place to be alone to think, reflect, and use his hands in productive activity. Using tools provided by his mother — hammers, nails, saw, wood, books, and so forth — he made things. Eventually Jason grew into a brilliant engineer. He'd developed amazing problem-solving skills, a firm grasp of spatial relationships, and manual dexterity while working in his own little world. Rather than withdraw, Jason independently sought out supportive neighbors and friends in a small town who helped him survive. As an adult, he was better able to relate to others and negotiate and collaborate on his way to a successful career.

The elements of successful negotiation and collaboration in adults are:

• *Active engagement in interpersonal problem solving.* You regard conflicting views as a challenge and consider solutions as opportunities. Rather than withdrawing, you face challenge head-on.

• *Assumption of personal responsibility.* You take charge of yourself. Your self-esteem helps you negotiate for the best for yourself. You aim high rather than lower in your requests and assumptions. And you seek to understand and maneuver the elements of the situation in order to reach a satisfying result for everyone. But you know that you are the one most responsible for looking out for your own needs and wishes.

• *Sense of personal safety.* You know how to find a safe place to recharge and regroup. You don't depend on anger to win in negotiating or collaboration. You only confide in others who are trustworthy and not crazy or destructive. Don't assume all those with whom you need to collaborate are on your side, even though they say so. Always be sure to speak for yourself when possible and never expect others to do everything right by you.

 • *Ability to think clearly.* You do not withdraw into circular thinking. Nor do you allow prolonged emotional reactions to major or minor setbacks to cloud your reasoning.

Can everyone learn to collaborate?

Yes! In fact, many people cannot be productive outside the structure of a group. Unsuited for isolated endeavors, they need the group process to fulfill their individual potential. Sometimes a chaotic or depressed childhood predisposes people to the need for the grounding and stabilizing structure of a group. Left alone, they become depressed or fantasize excessively or give in to fears that paralyze them.

Still other people are capable of functioning independently - once they get "started." They might lack the creativity to come up with the original concept. Or they may not have the confidence to begin work without getting encouragement — the "push" — from someone else.

Some can initiate a project, but they can't sustain the effort needed to finish it because they hate "detail." Defeated early in the implementation process, they flit from one concept to the next, never turning anything into a reality. They are great idea people - but they need to collaborate with others who can turn the ideas into a viable operation. Others can do everything alone, from beginning to end, but need people to acknowledge, congratulate and reward their efforts, or they don't feel they've truly achieved what they set out to do.

For these and other reasons, working and living alone isn't satisfactory or productive for many, perhaps most, people.

Some people, on the other hand, will not, cannot, or perhaps even should not join groups. They may be extremely introverted, severely ill or disabled, conditions which prevent them from getting together with others. Or they may be struggling with overwhelming personal problems, such as caring for terminally ill loved ones, caring for children alone, or barely getting through a traumatic divorce or a tax audit. Some jobs or professions require long periods of time alone, such as writing or research, athletic training, or work on computers. Inventors and designers and many others work essentially alone.

For whatever reason, people who are not involved actively and physically with groups still need feedback and can be collaborators in their own way. A writer may share his work with a mentor or another professional - and certainly depends on an editor's feedback and criticism to develop ideas into finished articles or books. Even Olympic athletes who compete individually have coaches. Increasingly, people who work alone on computers are turning to others in the same position through online services. Collaboration is essential if you're going to solve problems, meet your goals, and remain resilient.

The life of a lone entrepreneur or consultant has been glamorized in recent years — as has the life of a single adult. It's important to evaluate your strengths and weaknesses before deciding if you are suited for loner endeavors. Working alone requires high levels of tolerance for isolation and the ability to function independently with minimum feedback.

However you live and work — alone or in a group — you need the skills of negotiation and collaboration to remain creative, productive, successful and resilient over time.

CHAPTER EIGHT

FINDING YOUR COLLABORATIVE STYLE

e developed the following exercises to help you become more aware of your collaborative patterns. Your answers to these questions should help you get a clear picture of the way in which you work or live with other people.

EXERCISE #1: Check out your collaborative history

RECALL the way in which you have collaborated with the partners who have had significant impact upon your life.

For example, have you developed the same kind of collaborative pattern repeatedly or was the pattern with each important relationship different? Some of your partnerships might have been impossible from the beginning. Others may have been difficult, but were workable and ultimately rewarding.

What's Your Collaborative History?

Check Out Your Collaborative History			
Step One **Partner**	Step Two **Project/Goal**	Step Three **Process**	Step Four **Results**
Who were my partners?	What were our goals?	How did we work together?	Did we both get what we wanted?

Take a clean sheet of paper and draw a chart for yourself that is like the previous chart. Complete each column in as much detail as possible.

In each case, use the following questions to guide your evaluation. Add questions of your own as they occur to you. Take a hard look at yourself and your history of collaborative relationships in both your personal and professional life.

Then use the following way of reflecting upon your partnerships – both your personal and professional collaborations.

1. **PARTNERS:** *Who were my partners?*
   Describe them in detail in the following categories:
   * Personality: the way they handled conflict;
   * Thinking patterns (methodical, analytical, imaginative, big picture, one-liners);
   * Negotiating and collaborating styles (conservative, innovative, dynamic, positive, nit-picking, aggressive, leader, follower, critical, supportive).

2. **PROJECTS/GOALS:** *What were our goals?*
   Discuss and describe the project and/or goal.
   Ask yourself the following:
   * Were we both passionate about our shared project or goal?
   * Which one of us initiated the collaborative goal or project?
   * Whose ideas largely prevailed? Were any of my ideas or my partners ideas accepted? If not, ask yourself, why not?
   * How were the goals enriched, changed or developed through our collaboration?
   * What other resources (material or human) were necessary for us to complete this collaborative effort?

3. **PROCESS:** *How did we work?*
   Explore the effectiveness of the processes you used with the following questions:
   * How well did the two of us collaborate in our dealing with other people?
   * How did we work together? Frequency (occasional or often);

74

Intensity (casual or brain-storming); Intimacy (long-distance or joined-at-the-hip)?
* Did I assume the major function or role? If "yes" describe how. If "no", why not?
* How did I feel about my participation?
* Was the collaboration friendly, hostile, easy, difficult, contentious or supportive?
* Did we meet the deadline? If so, who was the driver and who followed? If not, why not?

4. **RESULTS:** *Did we both get what we wanted?*
Consider the results of your collaboration as you think about your partner, your projects and your processes and ask yourself the following questions:
* What was the outcome? Did we complete the project or leave it at mid-point?
* Would I work with this person again? Why? Or, Why not?
* Did it end feeling good or was there damage?
* What would I do differently?

Take a moment to reflect.
What was the most successful collaboration you ever had?
The least successful?

Identify the specific details of both so that you know what to do and what to avoid in the future. You may find it easier to separate your personal and professional relationships in checking out your patterns. Try to be as clear as you can be. To do that, you'll have to set aside some emotional responses. Maybe thinking about a relationship with a past co-worker or supervisor makes you angry or sad or embarrassed. Look objectively at what led to that feeling. The clarity of your insight about your collaborative patterns will affect your future collaborations.

How much have you learned from your own history? And how can you apply those lessons to future collaborative choices and behaviors?

What's your collaborative style?

Now that you've looked at your collaborative history, we'd like for you to analyze your collaborative style.

COLLABORATIVE STYLES:

We all encounter life in different ways at different times, each using our own unique style adapted to the situation and the people involved. STYLE is your signal to other people, telling them how you will deal with challenge or controversy, trauma or frustration. That signal tells them whether or not they can trust you in a crisis, whether they should follow you or run the other way.

Essentially, style is our resiliency thumbprint.

Style provides the basic unit of information about the way you operate in life, just as a fingerprint identifies your physical self. Try to identify your style from the descriptions below. We all vary our behavior in response to different people and different situations. Look for your most characteristic traits.

THE RISK TAKER

The risk taker embraces life on the edge. He or she looks for challenges and creates them when they are not there. Risk takers have little or no fear and tend to live spontaneously. If others don't quickly join them, risk takers tackle the project on their own. They become bored easily. Often they do not recognize those situations in which they need to change their style.

Their defeats are most likely to come when they cannot win or master the challenge. Yet, when they face a defeat, they let nothing stop them from getting up and starting again, even if they must use pure anger (internally) as their power source.

The biggest challenge to the risk taker's resiliency?

A series of failures can lead them to burnout, bitterness, and alienation. Those failures typically occur when they take risks which don't pay off, either because they can't maintain the commitment or finish the project alone or because they can't organize others to help them. Setback after setback causes them to spiral downward into withdrawal.

Risk takers can lose in negotiations if their proposals do not have substantial research and planning behind them. When that happens, they become isolated. If they work well with a team so others provide the "operations" and the "back up" functions, risk takers can thrive. As we have said before, no one can be successful and resilient over the long haul if they cannot work with other people.

THE DECISION MAKER

The decision maker is more cautious about life and less spontaneous than the risk taker. Gathering information, collecting experts, checking their "R.O.I." (Return on Investment), and planning their moves in a proactive manner, the decision makers do not fear challenge. They simply like to plan and strategize their moves before striking out. They usually want to make certain that they are prepared for the next challenge facing them. And, no one can do that better.

But those around the decision makers are often struggling unnoticed with their own inadequacies and unwillingness or inability to keep up with the plans foisted upon them. Group productivity can suffer unless the decision maker learns how to motivate people around him by giving them more participation in the decision making process. Decision makers often fail to do this, because they overestimate others' problem solving abilities. Being so good at it, they may assume others are that good too and overlook the struggles going on around them.

Or they may have a low opinion of others' capacities and intelligence because they believe themselves to be better at problem solving. That attitude keeps them from fully engaging the support of their staff or their family. Eventually the people around them may tell them only what they want to hear while withdrawing into obstructionism, insecurity or passivity.

The challenge to their resiliency?

Because they take so much responsibility for decisions, they often don't receive sufficient creative feedback. They may not attract the most creative people. With the full load on their own backs, decision makers
are prone to the burnout associated with excessive responsibility. The decision maker's resiliency is constantly being eroded without being replaced.

THE ANALYZER

The analyzer faces challenges with a firm grasp of the pros and cons associated with each response to them. Like the decision maker, she or he gathers information from every available source. Less extroverted than the decision maker, the analyzer tends to operate alone.

When faced with unexpected challenges, analyzers engage in protracted analysis, which is a delaying tactic. Because they may be isolated and hesitant, they are slow to make changes and make only conservative changes when they finally do move. Not prone to the bold stroke or the cutting edge choice, analyzers make conservatism, careful decision making, and loyalty their strengths.

What is the challenge to their resiliency?

Analyzers tend to limit their life experiences to those which do not require much risk taking, aggressive or extroverted behavior. While they may be resilient within limited boundaries, they are not resilient in circumstances and situations outside those comfortable areas. Over time, their safety space may grow smaller. Increasingly reluctant to push themselves outside that space, they lead restricted lives.

Analyzers compromise their resiliency by their behavior because social involvement and risk taking are fundamental to building resiliency over time.

THE INFLUENCER

The influencer has tremendous personal resources. They delight in having relationships. And, of all the styles, they can muster the most help, support, cash or other resources. They love people and challenges because they enjoy "fixing things." But, faced with the unfamiliar challenge, they either drift into being dictatorial or let others take care of the situation until it reaches crisis proportions when they finally step in.

The challenge to their resiliency?

They aren't self-starters. They are reliant on the quality of the group. If they can't find enough people to form the needed groups, they can't work effectively.

Influencers tend to work and socialize with people who are not quite as strategic or confident as they are. Therefore, they don't maximize their abilities through being challenged by equals. When they are placed in groups of people with equal or greater abilities, they often have problems in negotiating and collaborating. They may feel resentful or end up being excluded by the group. Influencers are typically always looking for the "perfect" group, in the belief that they will achieve their greatest potential in such a situation.

Influencers often fail to develop their own talents and skills, so suffer further loss of resiliency by not living up to their potential.

THE PEACEMAKER

Peacemakers face challenges by intervening in the action around them, not by bold initiative or planning. They are process-oriented and rarely create their own plan, program, or design. Inexperienced at risk taking, they approach life in a guarded way. Caring for others is a top priority with them. Peacemakers are not apt to challenge the system, but they are always trying to make the system work.

Not surprisingly, peacemakers often choose jobs in the service industry. Because they are more in tune with others than most of us are, they can deflect conflict, anticipate the needs of a client or customer, and smooth the path between dissenting group members. In personal and professional relationships, their astute awareness of "danger signals" communicated by others can also make them excellent enablers.

Their greatest strength is their wise use of time. Because they are immersed in the intricacies of group process, they do not waste time trying to break through barriers or attempting unwise or unfocused changes. They are already operating in "real time", so they can reorganize, reframe, redesign or intervene at the "stuck places," repairing personal systems quickly, with little loss of time.

The challenge to their resiliency?

Peacemakers become immersed in petty details. They struggle to make flawed systems work when they should be looking for alternatives. Their patience can turn them into Don Quixotes, always jousting with windmills. Peacemakers are firmly entrenched in the group. If the group grows, they grow along with it. But if the group falls apart, they self destruct. Also, their position within the group is typically near the bottom. More aggressive members rise to the top.

In the worst case scenario, peacemakers become depressed because their efforts are not fully appreciated and they do not receive just compensation for their talents. They may become cynical and even sabotage the group and/or themselves, leading to disaffiliation later in life. At that point, their greatest strength — immersion in a group — is lost. And, so is their resiliency. A peacemaker is only as resilient as the group.

THE ECLECTICS

The eclectics use whatever it takes to get the job done. They can be risk takers, decision makers, analyzers, influencers, and peacemakers depending on the role that is needed in the situation. Their greatest strength comes from their adaptability, which gives them a high level of resiliency. Eclectics are generalists who tend to work in management or self-employment, where they can perform a variety of functions.

Knowing they have internal resources, including confidence, self-esteem, and a balanced perspective to problem solving, eclectics KNOW they can face challenges and resolve difficulties. They have adopted a system of problem solving which works like this:

- *STOP.* They conduct a baseline assessment of worst case and best case scenarios and a general overview of the situation.
- *REFLECT.* They think about the short term and long term plans and all their implications.
- *RESPOND.* Now is the time to act in the following way:
  - *INVENTORY.* They list the external resources available to handle the situation and effect change successfully.
  - *CALL.* Once they have evaluated the resources, they start making calls to pull together the people and materials needed.
  - *ORGANIZE.* They organize the group or system assembled to solve the problem and make the change.
  - *MAINTAIN.* Once the new system is in place and change has been made, they may administer and manage the functions.

Eclectics shine in the area of maintaining systems. Their most apparent limitation is their tendency to become completely absorbed in one function or aspect of a problem while ignoring the others or delegating them to people who can't handle the challenge. Sometimes their approach to problem solving is superficial, too broad or general, and not marked by creative thinking.

The challenge to their resiliency?

In believing they have "everything covered," eclectics can close their minds to new ideas. They may not be as open to creative ideas as they appear to be. If successful, they can get stuck in their own success and fail to grow to new levels. It's hard to argue with success, isn't it? Yet golden handcuffs can keep one as securely in place as steel.

Eclectics trapped by their own success can fail to revitalize their creativity by holding too tightly to the methods that got them to the top. They may feel they have too much to lose to be innovative now. And often they fear the "young turks" coming along behind them. When that happens, they begin to lose their originality and risk-taking ability.

The greatest threat to an eclectic's resiliency is the creative stagnation that can follow repeated successes.

EXERCISE #2: Check out your collaborative style

Select the collaborative style that is most like your own from this list:

- ❏ RISK TAKER
- ❏ DECISION MAKER
- ❏ ANALYZER
- ❏ INFLUENCER
- ❏ PEACEMAKER
- ❏ ECLECTIC

Fill in the blank from the styles above and complete the following sentences:

My basic style is that of a _____
because_____
_____.

With authority figures (boss, board member, parent, etc.), I tend to be_____because_____
_____.

With my colleagues, I tend to be a _____
because_____
_____.

With my staff, I tend to be a _____
because_____.

With my family, I tend to be a _____
because_____.

With my friends, I tend to be a _____
because_____.

Can you change your style?

Some of the behavioral tendencies that influence style are just habit and habit can be changed. You are the person who determines how you live your life. We believe you can change your life and change your collaborative style. You make the decisions that determine how well you will bounce back from setback. You decide how you want to play the game of life and what you want to get out of it.

Often we pay little attention to the clues indicating our strengths and limitations — clues other people use to gauge their own responses to us. Be objective about your style, how it influences your approach to challenge, how it impacts upon your resiliency. If you ignore the clues now that they've been spelled out for you, you will probably stick with the style you've been using all your life, whether it works well or not.

The core tendencies that underlie collaborative style may be too imbedded in individual personality to be changed. For example, a serious intellectual who is committed to scholarship and study is not going to become an extroverted dealmaker. Our style is a lot of who we are.

But transformation happens every day. The domineering person learns to be more considerate. The shy person learns to speak out. These things can be changed through self-awareness and practice if you feel your style is a handicap in your life.

Take an honest look at your style. It is, as we've said, your resiliency thumb print, but unlike the print of your flesh, it can be changed.

PART THREE

RESILIENCY QUOTIENT:

CHECKING IT OUT

CHAPTER NINE

RESILIENCY QUOTIENT: CHECKING IT OUT

I n the preceding five chapters, you have learned about the four
areas of commitment necessary to resiliency: Perspective;
authenticity and conscience; hope and imagination; and negotiating and collaboration. How can you recognize which, if any, of the
four are problem areas for you? First, you can answer some questions honestly.

* Do you have central beliefs and values that help you gain
  perspective when you are struggling with tough problems,
  losses, crises? If someone were to ask your "philosophy of
  life," could you answer them?

* Are you usually authentic in your relationships, risking the
  exposure of your real opinions, thoughts and feelings when
  it's important to the situation?

* Do you feel normally hopeful about finding solutions to
  obstacles even if they aren't apparent at the time?

* Is your approach to problem solving proactive, drawing
  from a collaborative attitude? Do you stick your neck out
  and are you willing to make trades?

Have you defined your collaborative style now?

If you haven't, spend a little more time on the previous chapter.
And if you have — let's move on! In this chapter, you're going to
measure your resiliency quotient to determine how resilient you are.

We believe that the ability to collaborate well provides people
with a buffer against the loss of resiliency — which we call *burnout*.
Why? Successful collaboration requires a positive perspective,
authenticity, hope, imagination, and the practice of proactive
negotiation — all elements of resiliency. People who can put these
elements together in collaborative relationships are also resilient.
They continue to build resiliency, their own and that of others, as
they deal with life's challenges.

How resilient are you?

Do you believe that you are resilient? Very resilient? Somewhat? Only minimally? Are you afraid that you are so nonresilient that a setback — even one of less than critical proportions — could drag you so far down you won't be able to bounce back?

We can all place ourselves at some point along the resiliency scale. And most of us have moved from one end of that spectrum to another at different times in our lives. Where are you today? Is that where you want to be tomorrow?

Take your time in completing the resiliency quotient questionnaire below. Use the questions as an opportunity to think seriously about yourself. Don't feel pressured to "score" one way or another. Resilient people do not all face challenges in the same way. There are highly resilient introverts and extroverts, analyzers and influencers, decision makers and risk takers. There is no "right" or "wrong" style or way of being.

As you answer the questions, make note of the areas of commitment that you think need work if you're going to improve your resiliency quotient in the future. Only you can know where you are strong and where you need to develop. After you complete the questionnaire, you'll be able to answer the basic question:

How's your RQ?

RESILIENCY QUOTIENT QUESTIONNAIRE:

1. Do you have a problem-solving style that is mostly:
(A) Proactive
(B) Interactive
(C) Reactive

2. Is your usual relationship style mostly:
(A) Independent
(B) Interdependent
(C) Dependent

3. Most of the time, is your style of response:
(A) Aggressive
(B) Collaborative
(C) Passive

4. In a serious crunch, do you:
(A) Fight
(B) Turn to group support
(C) Withdraw

5. When a change of direction is needed, do you see it as:
(A) An interesting challenge
(B) Another problem to solve
(C) Indication that your life is a problem

6. Do you basically see yourself as a person who is:
(A) Positive and optimistic
(B) A realist
(C) Worried and pessimistic

7. Do you believe that you are generally:
(A) Goal-oriented
(B) Here-and-now oriented
(C) Past-oriented

8. Do you tend to see life as:
(A) Meaningful and purposeful
(B) "Just life," just the way it goes
(C) Rather meaningless and futile

9. Do you feel, most of the time:
(A) In charge of your own life
(B) The need to handle life to the best of your ability
(C) Out of control and overwhelmed

10. In your darkest moments, do you mostly turn to:
(A) Work and learning aids
(B) People and/or support groups
(C) Your own thought processes

11. **When you hit tough problems, do you find that your overall perspective is grounded in:**
(A) Your inner resources or "God within"
(B) The human community
(C) Fate, destiny, luck, past experiences

12. **When you are faced with a new challenge:**
(A) You get right to it
(B) You get to it in good time
(C) You procrastinate a lot

13. **Once you begin to tackle a problem:**
(A) You assault it until it's over
(B) You approach it methodically
(C) You give up too soon

14. **When you finally arrive at a solution to a problem:**
(A) You leverage it and take it to the next challenge
(B) You wrap it up and move on
(C) You feel relieved

15. **When you see something on your want list that is risky:**
(A) You go for it
(B) You weigh the wish against the risk and often go for it
(C) You dump the wish

16. **When things go wrong, do you generally:**
(A) Look at the big picture and tackle the obstacles
(B) Reassess to find something you could do differently
(C) Look for people to blame or blame yourself

17. **When you celebrate a victory, do you usually:**
(A) Feel like you deserve every bit of it
(B) Feel like it was the team that pulled things together
(C) Feel like a fraud

18. **When you suffer a defeat, do you usually:**
(A) Absorb it without much loss of self-esteem
(B) Examine your limitations carefully so it doesn't

happen again

(C) Get depressed and begin to doubt yourself

19. Do people turn to you as a resource because:
(A) You immediately help them tackle their problems
(B)   They know you would help them if they asked
(C) You would support any decision they made

20. All things considered, do you see yourself as:
(A) Unusually resilient
(B) Resilient enough
(C) Just limping along

When you have finished with the questions, think again.

Scoring the Resiliency Quotient Questionnaire couldn't be simpler. If you marked three-fourths of the questions with an A or B answer, you would score high on resiliency. All A's would suggest a hard-charging, optimistic approach to challenge but lacking some of the thoughtfulness and measured performance that is needed for "pacing and leveraging resiliency" suggested by the B responses. All B's would suggest consistency and tenacity in dealing with challenges but without some of the extra energy and fast responsiveness in the A responses that is often useful for sprinting and innovating.

If you marked three-fourths of the questions with a B or C response, you are likely struggling to recover from life's challenges as much as you are handling them. All C responses and you are likely to react too passively to be highly resilient. In either case, use insights, exercises and recommendations in this book to improve your functioning and your resiliency.

Were there times in your past when you believe that you were more resilient than you are now? Have you somehow lost your commitment to life? Do you feel that you haven't fully recovered from major setbacks?

Make a list of the things, people and habits that once sustained you. Have you let go of them? Lost them somehow? Make a decision to take them back - possibly in another form — and then do it. Maybe you can't repair old friendships but you can start new ones. Maybe you don't live near the wooded area where you walked to restore yourself in times of trouble — but you can find a new source of nature's restorative power, even in your local park.

You may remember longingly times in the past that felt magical and you think they can never be replaced. Think again! Neither the old friends nor the woods were magic in the first place. What you have lost are the automatic habits of friendship, of turning to nature or work or books or physical exercise to help you bounce back. You have changed your habits or perhaps your beliefs. You can change again. Yes, you can get back the feelings you believe are irreplaceable magic.

We have seen a workaholic client who danced in his youth rediscover both dancing and his sense of humor at age 48. We have seen midlife cynics who haven't made a commitment lasting longer than three years since they left home at eighteen get married for the first time, buy homes, adopt children — make promises for the indefinite future. We have seen many others find the "missing links" in their lives and then make changes they had been sure they never could make.

Resiliency is pure magic and it is within you.

PART FOUR

BOUNCING BACK

FASTER,

STRONGER,

SMARTER

CHAPTER TEN

BOUNCING BACK FASTER: GETTING STARTED

"**S** O YOU FAIL. SO WHAT." *Fortune* magazine, May, 1995. The cover story of that issue was about six business leaders who had bounced back from spectacular, and very public, failures. A photo of Sergio Zyman, the man who was behind Coca-Cola's disastrous product launch, New Coke, seven years ago, filled the left side of the cover. Looking down into the camera, mouth curved slightly, the once-fired Zyman looked thoroughly pleased with himself. And why not? In 1993, he returned triumphantly to Coca-Cola where he recently had his title expanded to chief global marketer.

Roberto Goizueta, the CEO, explained the thought process behind Zyman's rehiring by saying, "We became uncompetitive by not being tolerant of mistakes...You can stumble only if you're moving."

Zyman certainly has a reputation for moving. Known for unconventional thinking and risk-taking at top speed, he says his colleagues tell him, "Talking to you is like talking to a blowtorch." He believes most people don't respond as quickly as he does — and he's right about that.

Bouncing back faster - what do we mean?

Most people will never have Sergio Zyman's response time. Nor will they need to move quite that fast. By "bouncing back faster," we mean spending less time in doubt, insecurity or immobilization after a setback before moving on.

Obviously, some setbacks will require a longer bounce-back time than others. Zyman himself spent several years in low profile consulting work before returning to the glare of the corporate spotlight. Some time to reflect, recharge and retool is useful, even necessary, following divorce, job loss and other major life events. Single parents may find bouncing back fast particularly difficult because of the enormous demands placed on them.

On the other hand, many people get bogged down in the pencil-sharpening stage. After a setback, they tell themselves they will move on as soon as they have sorted the paper clips, sharpened the pencils, organized the closets, alphabetized the spices. Are you one of those people? And would you like to spend less time preparing the new plan before initiating and launching it?

We're going to teach you strategies for closing the time gap between setback and bounce back.

Strategies for bouncing back faster

1. Give equal weight to strategies in your personal and professional life.
Whole people have both personal and business commitments. To be truly resilient, you must develop both personal and work lives with equal effort and consideration given to goals, planning, self-discipline, accountability and commitment. Collaborative failure in either area of your life will inevitably slow you down in the other one.

Some points worth noting about personal strategies:

You can't formulate goals in your own mind alone. You must include the people in your life at work and at home in the planning process. Make creating routines that promote discussion of shared goals and responsibilities a priority at home — where they may not be as formally constructed as the way in which they are at work. Don't neglect your personal life. It won't run itself.

If you repeatedly dump your anger, fears, misery, pessimism and worries on your mate and family - you can't expect the collaboration to be successful. Family morale suffers when home is the place where you never put forth your best. Show your life partner the same consideration you show a client or the boss or the board of directors.

That old "ball and chain" concept of commitment is dated and obsolete. In the past, couples may have found that behaving as if their legs were tied together helped them face the world less fearfully. It doesn't work today, if it ever really did before. Commitment is not a drag on individual ambition. In reality, failure of commitment is the anchor that can drag you down.

Larger and larger numbers of families have both adults and even some children engaged in productive employment or dual careers. As a result, traditional separation of responsibilities putting one mate in charge of home and the other of employment works for very few families. Both partners have to function well in both areas, home and work, which makes communication essential. Children's increasingly demanding schedules require that they also be included in many family negotiations.

2. Develop a clear plan.

Strategies are plans made in steps, plans which have both form and flexibility. You can reduce further setbacks from false starts or dead ends and eliminate time-consuming unnecessary steps by making clear plans. If you don't take control of where you are going in the planning stage, you may end up somewhere not of your own choosing.

Arnold Brown tells a story: People function in a way that assumes they are standing in the middle of a river on a rock; suddenly, they discover they aren't on a rock at all, but on a raft and they are moving with the river. His point: You need to direct the course if you intend to get there.

We have heard clients describe situations in which change carried them along more or less without their consent or at least their full participation. They found themselves going down river when they hadn't even realized they were standing on a raft! That can happen to you if you don't stay awake and in control of your own destination — which requires vision.

Vision allows you to look ahead beyond tomorrow or next week and project your goal into the more distant future. With vision, you see that future as it can look if you develop and carry out a good plan. Vision clarifies our direction. And vision is tied into resiliency in a strong way. The commitment to life is a commitment to a future which can be made better than the present. Our country's founding fathers had vision, as do entrepreneurs like Bill Gates, Estée Lauder, Warren Buffet, Oprah Winfrey. The single mother struggling on a tight budget who manages to put some money aside for the children's college fund — or her own continuing education - has vision.

If you can't communicate your vision to someone in five minutes or less and get a reaction that indicates understanding — you aren't ready to move ahead. When you can say it, you can do it.

EXERCISE: Fantasy to develop vision

You can't have a vision or a plan — and you can't move fast - if you don't know what you love. And, sometimes people don't. See if you gain some insight into what you love by examining your fantasies. Reality is nothing more than fantasy with legs on it. Let's begin by making an inventory of possibilities. Under the following five columns, list everything that comes to mind.

Inventory of Possibilities

	Fantasies	Feelings	Assets	Liabilities	Contacts
Personal					
Professional					

FANTASIES: Be imaginative, wishful and hopeful.
FEELINGS: The ones you're experiencing now and most often, especially in the recent past.
ASSETS: Talents, aptitudes and resources available to you.

LIABILITIES: Behaviors and habits that limit your possibilities.

CONTACTS: People you consider to be helpful supporters, advocates or casual contacts who would/could offer possible links to change. Don't forget - these people know other people, too.

Further steps to develop your inventory of possibilities:

- List those things you feel most passionate about.
- List those things you find most interesting to do — at home, at work, at play.
- Indicate your needs and the assumptions you make about your life.
- Complete the following sentence: I absolutely do not want to

_____

_____

- How do you sabotage yourself — personally and professionally?
- Write a few paragraphs on the quality of life you wish to lead.

3. Solve problems in a new way.

Problem solving requires active thinking. Jeff Olson, a leading multi-level marketing executive and president of TPN, The People's Network, once told us that there are three ways in which you can learn to solve problems. He identified them as: <u>Learning knowledge</u>, such as seminars, audios, books and discussions. <u>Action knowledge</u>, or learning by doing. <u>Modeling</u>, which means emulating the behavior of others whom you respect.

Eva Langley jumped into the job as president of an executive out-placement firm from a staff position very fast, following a dramatic reorganization and downsizing. Overnight, the power base, philosophy and personnel of the company changed. With no time to draw a clear map, Eva leaped into Olson's "action knowledge" mode and began to learn by doing. Under her leadership, the company is past the fast start-up phase and into growth and consolidation.

What made the start-up successful? Eva describes her progress as follows:

1. Through continuous brain-storming with staff, she arrived at a company redefinition: What will the company look like? What real resources do we have on hand now?

2. The available resources were implemented immediately to provide a stable basis for immediate operation.

3. Gaps and missing resources were identified and immediate steps were taken to garner the missing pieces.

4. Eva decided on a dual-track program that included maintaining the existing company commitments to provide stability while launching a growth and development phase based on a personal passion for multi-media training programs. Drawing on previous contacts, she took full charge of the client relationships and the marketing needed to seed the growth program.

Eva is the first one to say that learning by doing creates overload.

Getting started fast provided opportunities for mistakes that might not have occurred if the pace had allowed for more advance planning. Overload also spilled into her personal life, forcing her to organize and plan times to relax and rest with her mate to compensate for the long hours. The discipline and problem solving she brought to her private and work life during the start-up period is what made it all fly.

Identify people you know or know about, people you consider good role models of resiliency. Describe their strengths.

4. *Affiliate and network with people who can help develop your vision and initiate or implement your plan.*

Your choice of associates, both personally and professionally, is critical to resiliency. You must select people and groups who fit the needs of the changes you want to make. Consultants, specialists, special purpose groups and associations — all can help you toward positive change and greater resiliency. In these group relationships, you will be giving back to them, too. This positive give and take builds resiliency for everyone involved.

Sometimes you have to let go of friends and business associates who have in the past only dragged you down. That doesn't necessarily mean you have to end those relationships. But you may need to limit your contact with these people, particularly during periods when you need to move fast to change. Hold on to those long-term relationships with people who support your positive changes rather than encourage you to remain the same.

We caution you to be selective about joining new groups or adding affiliations to your life. Some people in their zeal for change join too many organizations or volunteer for too many committees exposing them to different people. They can soon feel overloaded. And that feeling becomes an excuse for doing nothing. Pick and choose carefully.

Some people join groups for status. Others join to have something to fill their leisure time or because someone they know belongs and suggested they join. Many people care deeply about their groups because they represent causes. Some people only affiliate with those in the same industry or on the same socioeconomic level. Others don't belong to any groups because they fear involvement — which can cripple their ability to bounce back.

The following exercise will help you ask and answer the question: What can I give and what can I receive from this affiliation?

Affiliation exercise

Check your participation in the groups to which you belong by completing the following sentences. Are you active? Passive? Proactive?

1. I belong to _____(number) organizations.
2. They are: _____ (names and descriptions of professional and personal or social organizations.)
3. I have belonged to this group for _____ (years) _____ (months).
4. I have been _____(active)_____(inactive)_____(proactive).
5. I am willing to either drop this affiliation or become more active(describe plans) _____
   _____.

5. Use networking to bounce back faster.

Most people use networking as a form of socializing which can give them career benefits. Often, they see it as a one-way street, which is a waste of time, not a creative strategy. If you are always asking, "What can I get from this group, this person?" — you are wasting both your time and the group's.

We believe that you can utilize networking to support your own resiliency and that of others if you remember the following points we gleaned from Mel Kaufman, a visionary business relationship mentor:

• <u>Be prepared</u>. Choose which events to attend based on what you can learn and what you might be able to contribute. Decide in advance:

    -When to arrive
    -Whom you most want to meet
    -How to extricate yourself from a person who is wasting your time
    -What questions to ask

• <u>Try to spend 20 percent of each conversation exchanging productive information</u>. Information is power. What can you share? What can you learn?

• <u>Networking and "selling" don't mix</u>. Don't consider a networking function as a roomful of captive potential customers. Put your sales pitch away.

• <u>Assist others in fulfilling their dreams</u>. The old adage is really true: You help yourself by helping others. Supporting another's resiliency makes you more resilient.

• <u>Honor your commitments</u>. You gain in authenticity — and resiliency — by keeping your word.

6. Practice open and honest communication with the partner(s) you can trust.

"Communication" has become an overused word in our time — but don't let over-familiarity with the word stop you from taking this piece of advice seriously. You need to have trusting relationships where you can be clear about your goals, plans, assets and limitations. We have repeatedly seen the value of collaboration in resiliency. And you can't have a successful collaboration without open and honest communication.

Don't try to have this kind of relationship with people who have a history of not supporting you or, worse, betraying you. And don't try to have this kind of relationship with people whom you can't support as you expect them to support you. Listen carefully to the other person's needs before you enter into any kind of mutual support agreement.

Can you support them? Will they support you?

7. *Refuse to be passive in negotiating the necessary conditions of your recovery.*

Sometimes, you have to stick your neck out — and this is one of those times. If you're going to bounce back faster, you may have to do things which are not comfortable and familiar, such as asking for the help you need rather than waiting for someone to notice you need it. You will recover from hurts and misunderstandings faster if you are more proactive.

And most important, don't waste valuable time in withdrawal, pouting, stubbornly clinging to a polarized position, or silence. Act! Should discussion become bogged down, ask for a brief time out so that all parties can think about it. Set a date to reconvene and continue the discussion before everyone goes their separate ways. Follow through when the arranged time to talk approaches.

8. *Create a sense of urgency.*

You have to convince partners or your support team that there is a reason for moving fast. Marshall your facts and convey a sharp sense of the problems, costs and losses that are inevitable or likely if immediate actions aren't taken. Establishing this sense of urgency is necessary in creating a climate where quick response is not only possible but probable.

Cautions about making changes

Change won't last if you only change behavior and not your attitudes, beliefs and values. If you don't take care of the basics, you either won't bounce back fast or, following a superficial recovery, you will backslide to more familiar patterns.

1. Reassess your Resiliency Quotient (RQ) often.

Everybody's RQ fluctuates depending on the situation. If your RQ is less than it was, you may not be bouncing back as fast as you would like. Take more risks, without being reckless. If you're feeling depressed, get help. Don't try to fake enthusiasm you don't feel. And if your skills are inadequate, take action to improve them.

Sometimes when people aren't bouncing back quickly, they make unrealistic promises to themselves and others because they feel guilty about not moving or changing. Be careful about making promises based on guilt. You'll only feel worse if you let others and yourself down by breaking your word.

2. Develop your personal bank from which to draw when you need resources.

Our core beliefs, values, loves and hopes give us strength. They are like money in the bank, a savings account which we can draw upon to boost our resiliency when needed. Remind yourself regularly of those inner resources so you don't lose sight of your purpose for change. Draw upon them when you are wishing to fire your creative imagination.

3. Avoid the dry rot syndrome.

Dry rot happens to people who spend too much time in front of the television, or in bars, or sleeping. Unless you are exhausted from caring for the elderly ill or several small children or recovering from an illness yourself, you don't need to spend the weekend in bed with the remote control. If you feel the rot beginning, take action. Get up and walk around the house or the block. Pull out that list of fantasies you wrote. Speed walk with a friend. Get some help before launching any ambitious projects.

Now — Accept Change

Change is a permanent way of life! You can't avoid change. By accepting that, you bounce back faster.

1. Choose how you will change.

You can make choices about change, even if it is only to choose the attitude you will take toward a change foisted upon you. Rarely are people prisoners of their environments. You can alter your surroundings and circumstances by making changes, maybe small, maybe huge.

2. Change in small degrees.

Never underestimate the importance of a small change. If you see no way to pursue a proactive change at the moment, don't assume you have to remain stuck. Adapt through small corrections. They can make a big difference in your future.

For example, if you can't leave home to get a job, find some work you can do at home, such as word processing or home study. Or work on developing job skills. Anything you can do to improve yourself and the family finances will be a positive change.

3. Don't be stopped dead by a wrong change choice.

Sometimes the wrong choice slows people to a stop. Maybe they have lost their confidence to make a good choice. Or they feel guilty, demoralized, or even stupid for making the wrong move.

Learn from your mistakes. Don't let them stop you from moving on.

It's an act of maturity to go back and apologize, or to change your mind and admit it. Refuse to let pride hold you back when you need to clear the field to reenter the game.

4. Don't hang on to old choices out of loyalty.

Self-preservation is enlightened self-interest, not selfishness. Sometimes you have to cut old ties with people, companies, ideas, places. Hanging on to something that doesn't work anymore — a relationship or a job or anything else — from loyalty, fear, passivity or laziness costs you more and more all the time.

Yes, all commitments are imperfect. Only you can choose where to draw the line when something or someone fails to support you. And, if you can't get out, make adjustments, no matter how small.

5. Change is not a fad.

Some people equate change with trendiness. You may think that change signals either lack of integrity or an admission that whatever you did or wore or liked in the past was flawed.

Change is an ally, not the enemy. Continuously check your response to change. Is it positive? Do you see change as opportunity, excitement, newness, challenge? Or is your response negative? Do you see change as frightening, awkward, resented, too much work?

6. Find stability during change.

To avoid disorientation while changing, keep some elements of your life stable. People who have rituals at work or at home handle change more easily than those who don't. For some people, regular church attendance, special times shared with a partner or friend, even regular phone conversations provide that stability.

7. Reprogram those early messages that stall bouncing back faster.

Do your beliefs help increase your bounce back speed — or decrease it? Often people aren't even conscious of those messages they got in the past. Without understanding what they're doing or why, they repeat patterns that inhibit resiliency.

We were struck by the importance of these messages when we heard the story of two women, guest speakers at the same event. One requested a limo. The other took a train because it had not occurred to her to ask for a limo.

The woman who arrived in the limo believed in her own worth. As a child, she had suffered a serious illness. When a tyrannical nurse spanked her at a camp for chronically ill children, she told her mother, who believed her, packed her belongings, and took her home.

The other speaker had never learned to ask for what she needed. She'd spent her life waiting for people to notice what she needed or deserved — and to give those things to her.

The following exercise taken from Dr. Warschaw's book, *Rich Is Better,* will help you identify those messages and see how they impact on your ability to bounce back faster.

106

EXERCISE: Past Messages

Make three columns each for your life as a child and as an adult. List all the activities, pleasures, responsibilities, duties, even ways of thinking that seem important to you. Take your time.

As a child, I was ...

ALLOWED TO	REQUIRED TO	FORBIDDEN TO
_____	_____	_____
_____	_____	_____
_____	_____	_____
_____	_____	_____

As an adult, I ...

ALLOW myself to	REQUIRE myself to	FORBID myself to
_____	_____	_____
_____	_____	_____
_____	_____	_____
_____	_____	_____

Are you surprised at how much the messages given the child still influence the choices made by the adult?

Many of our choices, personal and professional, are influenced by those messages — as are our attitudes toward change. Don't accept the old childhood messages as gospel. Say NO to those inhibiting rules that make no sense in adulthood and that get in your way.

Profile of a recovery

"I got into business with the wrong partners," says Johnny Lewin, who bounced back from a tremendous loss. "Though my three partners were young in years, they had gotten 'old' on the job. They would never educate themselves. As a result, we didn't get involved in desktop publishing when we should have. And they were not sufficiently committed to success."

Their advertising agency was handicapped at the start by being undercapitalized. And the partners dug their hole deeper by not catching the wave of technological change fast enough. Still, Lewin kept trying to "fix" the company by selling faster, working more hours, borrowing more money. At one point, he formed another ill-considered partnership between his firm and two other companies. Johnny had been trained in loyalty and responsibility "through thick and thin" in his youth — a rule that was so ingrained it governed him into his fifties.

"Then I had a heart attack," he recalls. "While I was in the hospital my partners got additional bank loans and I ended up being stuck with another $100,000 of debt."

His bankers told him they would continue to back him if he got rid of his partners. But Lewin didn't have the "heart" to abandon them. He stayed too long in his professional relationships and lost everything.

Having heart is a good thing — but giving away your heart is not. Hiring a friend or making a friend of your employee can land you in the tar pit of "niceness." You may want to be so "nice" that you assume too much responsibility for other's welfare.

When the flight attendant instructs passengers, "Place the oxygen mask on your own face first before placing the mask on your children," he or she is telling you — You won't be able to help your children if you can't breathe. Lewin gave everything, when he should have been ensuring his own supply of oxygen.

"I waited too long to move," he admits. "I wasn't resilient. But I learned a lot from that experience."

One of the lessons: Someone else is better suited to be president of the company. Lewin convinced his live-in partner, Diedre Williams, that she should become president of his new company, formed after the old one collapsed. Twenty years her senior, Lewin was and is her mentor. Yet theirs is a close communicative relationship, a true partnership.

"I listen to her," he says. "She is more often right than wrong. She has earned my absolute respect. I am the shadow in this business."

As a team, Lewin and Williams are comfortable allowing each to lead when appropriate. Her resiliency has enabled him to grow in resiliency. By taking over much of the operational responsibility, she allows him to experiment with ideas. When she feels overloaded, she goes to him and asks, "How would you handle this? Give me another point of view."

Working together as a team is enabling them to respond more quickly to change, to bounce back from setbacks faster.

What do people who bounce back faster have in common?

People who run fast share the following traits. They:
- Know what their responsibilities are — and what responsibilities really belong to someone else.
- Are optimists — and realists, too.
- Realize that failure contains possibilities — lessons learned, the seeds of future success, the opportunity to grow in resiliency by bouncing back.
- Don't waste a lot of time on negative thinking.
- Celebrate the gains rather than mourn the losses.
- Move on once they know it's over.

Let's get real

As pragmatists, we know that no matter how fast, strong, or smart you are — you will occasionally find your resiliency seriously stalled by life conditions that resist all of your efforts to change.

Some people, no matter how much they attempt to bounce back fast, may not be able to move that quickly. They may have family responsibilities which demand time and energy. Many single parents, for example, are not able to bounce back as quickly as those without children or those who have partners to help them raise children. There is only so much time in a day!

We encourage you to examine the roadblock to change carefully before you conclude you can't get around it. Maybe you can — if you move a little more slowly this time. Examine your options regarding change and ask: *What's it going to cost me in the long run if I don't change?*

In his book, *Tough Minded Faith,* Robert Schuller says that "possibility thinkers" have the capacity to believe in all things. By that, he means:

* They see opportunities in obstacles.

* They believe that a stumbling block can become a stepping stone.

* They believe that frustrations can become meaningful forces to guide you along the right path.

* They believe that God uses both the good and bad experiences to mold, motivate and educate.

CHAPTER ELEVEN

BOUNCING BACK STRONGER: KEEPING IT GOING

*T*wo colleagues of ours, Emily Koltnow and Carole Hyatt, have run a number of workshops on career changes, mostly for women. In an exercise that they have found useful in getting the group started, they ask an attendee what her last job title was and what skills were needed for the job. One woman said she was a vice president of a public relations firm, which utilized communication, marketing, and people skills.

"What other career might utilize those skills?" Emily and Carol asked the group.

Women called out: marketing executive, advertising executive, human resource executive.

"Bartender!" said Edie Weiner, a dear friend of ours.

The group laughed. Then they understood the response. To have resiliency, you can't always do more of the same. You have to be willing to look at realistic, exciting, and *unexpected* alternatives. Most of us have hardly scratched the surface in thinking about the options open to us.

Weiner, a futurist and president of Weiner, Edrich, Brown, Inc. spends a great deal of time looking at the new and alternative options open to people as the economy changes.

"Many more executives who had been earning six-figure salaries are quitting to become personal trainers or chefs or bed-and-breakfast owners," she says. "But these people do not see themselves as servants now. They see themselves as being of service." This is also a choice being made by people who are forced out of their lucrative jobs.

Bill Strickler, who had a career in the shoe business for 39 years, is an example of creative change. A polished, knowledgeable retailer, he owned three successful shoe stores before selling them to become a sales representative for a large company. Then came the retail recession of 1991-92. Abruptly, he found his job terminated by the company's reorganization. He had become another victim of corporate downsizing. End of career.

But Strickler had a supportive family, some savings, and resiliency. He decided to build a new business around his hobby — bird-watching — and his commitment to nature, hiking, and conservation. "Wild Wings Unlimited," a wild bird nature center for birding enthusiasts, is now thriving near a ski slope in Big Bear, California. His wife, Jean, was recently able to leave her job which helped keep the family and business afloat and join him.

How did Strickler keep going through the three difficult years he calls "a rough transition?" Focus, hard work, and commitment — and the continued support of his family. He bounced back from setback, not only faster, but stronger, transferring extensive retailing savvy from urban shoes to country birding. And why not?

What do we mean by bouncing back stronger?

When you bounce back stronger, you keep resiliency going on a continuous basis. You don't come back from a setback and remain in that safe place. Rather, you keep moving and growing and changing — adapting to each new setback with greater resiliency. Your resiliency muscle keeps getting stronger with repeated use.

You have chosen change and made the first step in a new direction. The initial exhilaration is inevitably replaced by at least some anxiety — because choosing change certainly doesn't mean you won't face a significant challenge again. In fact, you will. And sooner rather than later.

In her work with corporations and in private practice, Dr. Warschaw runs programs and seminars to help people come to grips with the need to face transition. When they make the choice willingly and with an optimistic eye to who they can become because of what they love to do, both the individual and the employer are well served. But when the choice is seen as second best, as a step down or back, not only does the executive's spirit and resiliency shrink, but the employer also faces lowered morale on the part of all those who leave and even those who stay behind.

How equipped are you to deal with the *next* challenge?

Everyone perceives a challenge differently. What is hard for another may be easy for you and vice versa. That is one reason why collaboration is so beneficial to the success of any project. Your approach to problems and challenges — more than the problems and challenges themselves — affects your resiliency. To keep resiliency going on a continuous basis, you must adapt, adjust and solve problems constantly.

You will bounce back stronger and keep your resiliency going and growing in the face of new challenges if you are:

- Confident enough to speak or be silent.
- Creative enough to perceive and explore options.
- Resourceful enough to find support and information.
- Courageous enough to do what is uncomfortable.
- Disciplined enough to sustain good habits.

Handling the tough challenges - and the proverbial "last straws"

Philip Hanley is a creative photographer who went through a painful divorce and a job loss all in the same year. Worse, the job he lost had been a dream job. He'd left one company where the boss motivated people through "negative criticism" and kept telling him he would never be published on the magazine's cover. Finally, Philip went to another company which paid him twice his original salary - only to see that company fail within two years. His choice for change turned out badly. Yet, he didn't let this setback defeat him.

Hanley did something few people would think of doing. He went to the first boss, convinced this man that he should hire him back at twice the money he'd been making when he left there *and* be given greater opportunity and responsibility. How did he manage this?

1. He waited six months before calling.

2, He called his old boss to wish him a happy holiday.

3. He was invited over to visit.

4. He and the publisher discussed his reasons for leaving.

5. He convinced the publisher to give him a cover break.

"It took determination, persistence — and the willingness to stick my neck out," he says. Today he is responsible for eight out of ten covers.

Obstacles like the bankruptcy of an employer which appear to be major obstructions to progress are the tough challenges. Sometimes they seem to fill the road ahead of us like immovable boulders. Most of us eventually handle these challenges, even if they are big catastrophes like total financial collapse or an earthquake that destroyed the house. In the face of calamity, we are able to summon inner strength and marshall the resources of others to help us.

One of the biggest challenges to resiliency is handling the daily problems, the little stuff, or the "last straws" — those small setbacks and annoyances and defeats that chip away at your self-confidence the way drops of water eventually erode rock. You get in an automobile accident on the way to work and handle the immediate crisis just fine. Days later, after filling out the accident report, dealing with the mechanic repairing your car and the auto leasing agent supplying the interim rental car, you find that getting the last piece of information required by your insurance agent puts you over the edge. You slam down the phone and snap at the dog.

We all have those moments. Some people recover and move on to the next day of challenges more easily than others because they have developed stronger resiliency. The attitudes you need to bounce back stronger are:

- Know what you do matters.
- Know what you say has impact.
- Know how you behave has consequences.
- Know there are always moves to be made and you are solely responsible for yours.

• Know your own worth.

If it sounds like we're talking about personal accountability and discipline as a source of strength — you're right. We are. Bouncing back stronger requires commitment to the twin pillars of discipline and excellence.

Discipline

"Discipline is doing what you don't want to do," says a colleague of ours, "on the days that you don't want to do it, but you do it anyway."

Discipline is regular, frequent, and systematic — and includes what many people hate the most, routine. The 12-step programs are talking about discipline when they say, "90 percent of life is showing up." We would add — not just showing up, but being fully present and awake, too.

People who are unambivalent in their commitment to life have an inner discipline that keeps them focused in the face of distractions. They assume responsibility for themselves. Unlike those who blame others for their mistakes or claim victim status, they make no excuses.

Dr. Barlow's practice supports many highly creative professionals who see regular consultation or therapy as an important cornerstone of their continuous commitment to excellence and achievement.

Excellence

"I always understood that there is inevitably a solution," says Dr. Gina Luria Walker. "The quest for solutions develops resiliency. Knowing that helps you face your stretch in the desert — the period in which you must stick it out, hunkering down alone, to find the solutions. Resiliency is taking the props away from yourself and not accepting boundaries to what you can accomplish."

Many people believe that only excellence will survive in the next century. In an increasingly competitive work environment, being adequate may not be good enough to secure a decent living for a lifetime. Our nation's young people are growing up under the pressure of that realization.

Like other observers of the business scene, Dr. Gary Ranker, President of Transinfo, Inc., sees the need for resiliency growing in the twenty-first century.

"Twenty years ago, resiliency was toughness, survival," he says. "It involved brute strength. That has changed. Now, the future is unpredictable. The standards for employment keep getting higher. It's as if the bar is constantly being raised. Someone will always run faster, perform better.

"I am appalled that 28-year-olds worry about being dumped by their employers in a few years for 'sharper shooters.'"

A team of nine academic superstars from John Marshall High School in Los Angeles recently won the U. S. Academic Decathlon for the second time in eight years — and also shattered previous scoring records.

"We set this goal for ourselves a year ago, so we've been operating on the idea of delayed gratification and finally it's come," said Marshall's James Evrard, 17, who also won top individual honors at his level, in an interview with the *Los Angeles Times*.

In the same article, several students detailed the rigorous study schedule and personal sacrifice that led to their championship. They had given up social lives and hobbies to study eight hours a day, six days a week, for ten months — after completing regular classwork.

"At times you get mad and you don't like it because everyone around you is having fun, but in the long run it pays off," said Doug Kleven.

Most of us will never be able to make that kind of commitment to a single goal. We can, however, strive for excellence. What can you do to make the goal of excellence part of your bounce back strategy?

• Accept complete responsibility for your ongoing education and continuous learning. Don't wait to be told that you need to learn new skills.

• Reflect upon how what you are doing serves you. Your actions must be congruent with your purposes.

• Remember your destination and purpose — and never lose

sight of what you are trying to accomplish.

• Avoid people who are dream-stealers and will hold you down. These are the people who can't see how a new idea or a bold approach could possibly work. Barry Diller, whose genius had impact on ABC's Movie of the Week, the TV miniseries, the QVC Home Shopping Network, and Fox broadcasting network, has been quoted as saying: "Every time I ever did anything, everyone said it was gonna' fail. Every time."

• If you're not as fast as others or have too many other responsibilities to run at the head of the pack, know that keeping it going to the end of the race is winning, too.

Remember the story of the tortoise and the hare? There is a difference between "sprinters" and "long-distance runners." Discipline, tenacity, persistence and endurance compensate for speed. And making intelligent choices about which races to run also affects your ability to bounce back stronger.

Establish priorities

Each day you must decide which tasks are crucial and which can be delayed. The ability to prioritize is fundamental to building stronger resiliency. You can't do everything, all at the same time. Some people try and end up accomplishing nothing. Others take on whatever task is close at hand or being pressed on them by someone else without evaluating its importance. Learn to discriminate.

Often people become overwhelmed while trying to keep their bounce back going because they have forgotten that they have four choices and DO is only one of them. The other three are delay, delegate and dump. Look closely at your appointment books and calendars. How are you living your life? Are you doing things which should be done by others - or not at all?

Now take your to-do list for today and decide what really might fit in the following categories:

1. **DELAY.** The tasks that are not immediate.

Is this truly necessary? And if so, is it truly necessary today?

What is the real deadline on this? Can it wait? If the answer is No, it can't wait, then DO it. Otherwise, assign this task a priority ranking and do it another day.

2. **DELEGATE.** The tasks which can be done just as well — or better — by someone else.

Don't fall into the trap of believing only you can get the job done. Ask: "Must I perform this task or can it be done by someone else?" If it can, then delegate the job to your partner, boss, staff, friend, child, parent, or anyone else capable of assisting you. Don't set yourself up for failure, however, by giving it to someone who can't follow through.

Sometimes people assume responsibilities which aren't part of their job description. Some managers try to micromanage by telling subordinates *how* to perform the tasks they assign. And many of us, particularly women, take on more than our fair share of the household chores. Insist on setting fair boundaries and sharing responsibilities even if you encounter resistance.

3. **DUMP.** The tasks which really don't need to be done.

Strictly limit or get rid of tasks which are not moving you toward your goals. Streamline your office procedures and work methods. And apply the same techniques to your personal life.

4. **DO.** Some things really are necessary.

You have to walk the dog, file your income taxes, complete the tasks in your job description. You want to read that novel, exercise regularly, spend time with your family. The wants and musts will become more apparent after you have sorted out what can be delegated, dumped or delayed.

Your wake-up call

We have developed the following exercise as a wake-up call for people who have little awareness of their use of time and how to prioritize.

ANALYSIS OF YOUR LIFE CHOICES

I

**REALITY CHECK ON
TIME USAGE**

II

**MOMENTS OF
ENJOYMENT**

III

**FANTASY OF THE
GOOD LIFE**

IV

**WHAT ARE THE
TRADE-OFFS?**

EXERCISE: Analysis of your life choices

1. Make a time pie.

Your pie contains 24 hours. Divide it into activities — i.e., work, phone calls, socializing, watching TV, exercising, eating, sleeping — and the time spent arguing, feeling angry, depressed, regretful, etc. Include everything you do even if you don't do it every day.

Most people are shocked when we show them their pies. Did you realize this was where your time is going?

2. Moments of enjoyment.

How much of that pie represents time you have spent doing things you love? Which fulfill you? How much time spent nurturing, inspiring, enjoying others?

Ask yourself: What do I enjoy? If you say you enjoy walking, visiting with friends, reading and you have spent less than an hour a week on those activities — ask yourself, Why?

3. Fantasy time.

Create the pie that best represents your fantasy of the good life. Ask yourself: How would I really like to live my life and spend my time?

4. Trade-offs.

Compare your two pies. What are you willing to remove from the reality pie to make room for some pieces of fantasy pie? Can you let go of some of the activities which give you grief?

This analysis can be painful. You may realize that you are spending more time with negative people than you like — or spending more time at work than is necessary — or watching much more TV than you thought you did. And now you have to ask, Why? And, how can I replace those activities with ones I would more enjoy?

Are you willing to make a trade-off?

Don't deplete your energy by giving extra time to things you hate to do or completing endless tasks that have little to do with your job and nothing to do with your passions. Exhaustion will override resiliency. And you will probably need all your strength to deal with those bosses, subordinates, and partners who, consciously or not, try to sabotage your efforts to bounce back by their words and actions.

Counter outside threats to resiliency

Luke Cochran is a dynamic, funny and bright young marketing executive who left one job because he had a tyrannical boss (a man.) He looked forward to working for Jennifer — until he found her to be the same kind of boss. She demeaned him in public, embarrassed him in front of clients, and ridiculed his fun-loving style. No matter what Luke did, Jennifer found fault.

This time he didn't walk away from the job. He bounced back stronger by actively handling Jennifer and her threat to his resiliency. He enlisted the support of a mentor, another woman, who let Jennifer's boss know how she was treating her employees. Then he asked clients to write letters of support "for the record." He became more visible within the organization by speaking up at group meetings, volunteering for projects, attending social events. And, finally, Luke learned how to confront Jennifer's verbal abuse.

Verbal abuse is the initial and most commonly used competitive method — both in the workplace and at home. Sometimes it is strategic, conscious and deliberate. And sometimes people, who are stressed and frustrated, unintentionally lash out at others. Verbal abuse is the principal way we all express our anger and frustration. Who hasn't said something they later wished they hadn't?

There are different types of verbal abuse: humiliation, sarcasm, insult, battering, contempt, silence — all of which have impact, and in some cases, lasting impact upon resiliency. If you let verbal abuse chip away at your self-esteem, you become a "volunteer" — allowing your own abuse — not a victim. You have to take responsibility for your part in the situation to make it stop.

How can you handle verbal abuse?

• Recognize that it exists in both the home and the workplace. There is no safe space. And acknowledge its dangerous ability to destroy self-esteem. Words can and do hurt.

• Draw a mental line about how far you are willing to let another person go verbally before you say, "Enough!"

• When you can, confront the issue directly. Say, "I feel angry when you talk to me in that manner. Please find another way to tell me what you want from me and I'll do my best to take care of it." Try to arrange a time for a discussion when both of you are calm.

• When you cannot confront or the other person is unwilling to change and the level of abuse is intolerable — get ready to leave. Knowing that you are in the "readiness to leave" stage can increase your resiliency.

• If a friend is the abuser and you are not able to speak, leave immediately. Don't sit still and listen.

• Use your self-esteem as a buffer against hurtful words. Don't internalize the abuse. But realize that most people suffer severe damage under sustained abuse. This is a coping tactic, not a way of life.

Resiliency and reassessment

You can bounce back stronger by continually reassessing your resiliency. We have developed a series of exercises to help you reflect on your RQ so you can know if you are really bouncing back with the strength you would like.

Many people believe that resiliency is hanging on to a situation, job, or relationship — seeing it through to the end. Angela Ruiz, for example, wanted to make a success of her sales career so badly that she stayed in an impossible job in a company led by an extremely hostile and contemptuous man for two years before finally leaving. Real resiliency is keeping your options open and knowing that leaving is one of the options. Periodically ask yourself, "What do I really think? Is this really working for me?"

123

✳

EXERCISE #1. Resiliency reassessment

Remember, in chapter three, we talked about the three stages of resiliency — Holding on, Letting go, Moving on. Now, describe two situations in which you currently find yourself:

HOLDING ON: (To old business, old relationships)

LETTING GO: (Making a conscious decision that the old way doesn't work.)

MOVING ON: (Creating options with an eye to the future.)

If you can't think of two situations, it's time to pause, go back to chapter three — and read it again!

EXERCISE #2. Resiliency reassessment

Define resiliency:

Describe three business and/or personal situations in which you have been resilient:

1.
2.
3.

Describe three business and/or personal situations in which you might have been more resilient.

1.
2.
3.

Describe what you could have done differently to be stronger.

1.
2.
3.

Let's get real

You can't reassess if you're lying to yourself about your goals and priorities — or about what you're willing and able to do to make them happen. Check your honesty here. Be objective about your contributions and those of others.

Talk straight to the people in your life. Let them know what you're thinking and address problems before they become entrenched. And remember the other part of communicating is listening. You must be as willing to hear as you are to express feelings and opinions.

Conflict is inevitable when you're moving fast and strong. The next time you trip, remember: The only people who never fall down are the ones who aren't moving.

CHAPTER TWELVE

BOUNCING BACK SMARTER: GOING TO THE NEXT LEVEL

"Resiliency begins with self-esteem," says Doug Lawson, an international fundraiser for profit and non-profit organizations. "People who have low self-esteem have no faith in anything. Faith begins with love of self, then of God and others."

Lawson is also a minister, an author and an entrepreneur. He has bounced back from divorce, cancer, and a heart problem. In his darkest hours, he has always believed he could meet any challenge. And he has found his true calling in fundraising.

"If there is no resiliency, there is no generosity," he says. "People have to get out of the poverty mentality and know that they have a right to have and enjoy money. When they do that, they can be generous, too."

Lawson believes in leveraging self-esteem. By that, he means people with high self-esteem can afford to take risks, to be generous, to make dramatic changes — because they have their self-esteem like money in the bank backing them. On the strength of that philosophy, he bounces back faster, stronger and smarter from every setback.

Doug Lawson takes resiliency to the highest level in his life. You can, too.

What do we mean by bouncing back smarter?

At some point during the learning curve of any new task, you realize you "get it." You understand the details and comprehend the principles involved. Whether the task being learned is a physical or mental exercise, you suddenly know you can do it without making a great effort. Performing this exercise has become something you do naturally. And so it is with resiliency.

When you realize you are bouncing back smarter, you have begun to consolidate the changes you've been making and have reached the next level: transformation. Yes, you will continue making situational changes. The changes are not the transformation. They are only the evidence of it. Transformation — the ability to bounce back from setback not only faster and stronger, but smarter — is the altered mindset that occurs after the habits of resiliency have become stable and permanent.

The resiliency mindset

In life, nothing is permanent. And, in our time, as we have discussed in earlier chapters, the speed of change - the acceleration of impermanence — has created a great need for individual as well as societal resiliency. For example, there have been dramatic changes in the landscape of American business in the past decade. Words like "reengineering" and "downsizing" have entered our vocabulary.

The challenge to the mind now is recognizing, understanding and adapting to these changes quickly — and that often requires "unlearning" old behaviors and attitudes before learning new ones. In fact, such challenge requires a new mindset. We call this model of development — that includes the process of unlearning, learning, applying and modeling — the resiliency mindset. The continuous process is illustrated in the following diagram:

RESILIENCY MINDSET

```
              ┌─────────────────┐
         ────▶│   UNLEARNING    │────┐
        │     └─────────────────┘    │
        │                            ▼
┌───────────────┐            ┌───────────────┐
│               │            │               │
│   MODELING    │            │   LEARNING    │
│               │            │               │
└───────────────┘            └───────────────┘
        ▲                            │
        │     ┌─────────────────┐    │
        └─────│    APPLYING     │◀───┘
              └─────────────────┘
```

How the resiliency mindset works

A. Unlearning.

The process of unlearning takes place before you can learn a new way of thinking or behaving. The more strongly you believe that there is just one correct viewpoint or solution, the more difficult it will be to unlearn the old ways and open your mind to new ones. Unlearning doesn't invalidate previous knowledge — but transcends it.

How do you know when something should be unlearned? You have to be alert to the clues that your way of thinking, working or behaving isn't keeping up with the changes in your environment. A journalist who still uses a typewriter, for example, is limited by his own rigidity.

B. Learning New Ways.

Now you are ready to learn new ways of doing things. Organizations face this process on a daily basis. If they don't, they lose ground in the highly competitive business climate. Wait too long to learn new ways and risk becoming extinct like the dinosaurs. This is true for individuals as well as companies.

C. Applying What You've Learned.

Applying what you've learned is central to the development of resiliency. At some point, we all have to put down the books, walk out of the seminars, and start practicing our new skills. As you do that, keep looking toward the future and continually reassessing how these skills will help get you there.

D. Modeling.

While you are performing new skills, you serve as an inspiration and guide for those who are following your lead. Gauging the response of others is also an important form of feedback for you. When you inspire another person, their enthusiasm further inspires you.

Smart risk taking is a part of modeling. Whether you work for yourself or a corporation, you need to develop the resilient entrepreneurial spirit.

Using the resiliency mindset

After decades in the psychotherapy business and at age 60, Dr. Marguerite Simmons is now learning new ways of developing her business. Like other psychotherapists, she discovered in recent years that simply hanging out her shingle and waiting for clients no longer works as a business strategy. Changes in insurance coverage and employee benefit packages as well as the growth of the psychotherapy industry have worked together to create a climate in which therapists — like entrepreneurs — must deliberately market their services.

"I networked during the years when that was the preferred way of building a practice," she says. "It is no longer very effective, so I have adapted to the electronic age."

Using faxes, E-mail, multimedia presentations and other components of the information superhighway, Simmons has ventured into electronic marketing and restructured her client contact system.

"It is necessary to link and partner now in order to get referrals that were easier to come by in the days of networking," she says. "Linking and partnering are processes that ask the question, 'What can we do together?' — rather than, 'What can you do for me?'"

Simmons has a thriving practice at a time when other professionals don't because she has caught the wave of the future — collaboration. She was willing to unlearn old habits and learn new ones. "The key issue," she says, "is doing it, not talking about it, just doing it."

How can you develop a resiliency mindset?

Cultivate the habits which support a resiliency mindset and make them a permanent part of your life. You need to:

1. **Listen to your inner voice.** It is the bedrock of your self-esteem. Make consulting that voice an automatic part of your daily life. If you ignore the voice, risk losing your authenticity — and resiliency.

2. **Know there are choices to be made.** This is particularly

important when you are unhappy, when you are feeling trapped by circumstances seemingly beyond your control, when your responsibilities seem awesome. Start looking for solutions.

3. Learn to compliment. When you must criticize, do so constructively. There is a difference between constructive criticism and negative feedback. The former allows you to grow, while the latter kills creativity, productivity, and stifles the desire to communicate.

4. Be honest. Lies chip away at your self-respect. You cannot grow in resiliency without honesty in your daily communications with others.

5. Take creative risks. Push the boundaries! Welcome problems as the opportunity for creative problem solving. To stay creative, don't spend too much time on a problem once you have the solution in motion. Move ahead.

6. Create strategic alliances. Find partners you can trust. And remember that partners may not necessarily be personal friends. Alliances work best when the partners have common needs as well as goals. They don't work when one is expected to do something they're incapable of doing — when one wants something another cannot give — or when members of the alliance are envious of one another.

7. Be a leader when you can. Step up to responsibility in the absence of a boss, teacher or coach. Believe that you have leadership ability and take charge when needed.

8. Inspire your support team. As a leader, motivating and selling your colleagues and staff or family and friends is fundamental to group functioning. Nothing works well without it. Always reward others for the behavior you want to endure.

Portrait of a resiliency mindset

Six years ago, with a background in university teaching, administration and business, Dr. Gary Ranker started Transinfo Inc., an executive coaching firm that works with top-level executives at major corporations. In his coaching work, he has seen people who run the gamut from very resilient to nonresilient. And he can tell almost immediately that some people *won't* be resilient during change — and will present a resiliency-building challenge to him.

We asked Dr. Ranker what he felt makes people resilient during a corporate reorganization.

"The most difficult people to coach are the ones who talk about change and know they have to change and are trying to change — for all the wrong reasons," he says. "They talk about change, but they don't do it.

"My greatest failure was with a chief financial officer who only wanted the job because he didn't know what else to do. When he came to me, he knew his job was in trouble and he wanted to save it to salvage his lifestyle. He wasn't suitable for the job and eventually did lose it."

Other people who are difficult to coach include those who are overly sensitive to criticism, or have limited social skills, or feel "misunderstood."

The executives who *are* resilient during change share common traits and behaviors. He says they are able to:

• Take control of situations easily.

• Step away from a problem and look at it unemotionally.

• Assess "what's in it for them" — while acknowledging the needs of others and the implications of any particular solution for them.

• Detach and compartmentalize by breaking the needed changes into manageable pieces so they aren't overwhelmed.

• Envision a plan of action.

Even people with seemingly large problems can overcome them and grow in resiliency if they possess these attributes.

For example, Dr. Ranker says, "I worked with a CEO who initially had no awareness of how people were reacting to him. He was so out of touch with other people that he didn't know his staff was demoralized by his tactics and behaviors. But, he was able to realize that and use the coaching situation to help objectify his problem. He stepped away from it, analyzed the situation, broke it down into doable parts — and fixed it. He changed the tyrant he had been into an effective leader."

Like other observers of the business scene, Gary Ranker sees the need for resiliency growing in the twenty-first century.

Fine-tuning resiliency

We believe that people who reach the transformation stage pay more attention to nuances than others do. A nuance is the subtle yet pervasive shading of meaning conveyed by both verbal and non-verbal cues. The cues can either confirm or belie your conscious intentions and send warning signals about another's stated intentions.

There are two parts to human behavior: the conscious, the obvious, the stated; and the verbal and non-verbal nuances, which are more subtle. Ralph Waldo Emerson said, "What you do speaks so loud, I cannot hear what you say," — which is a more poetic way of expressing something your mother probably told you more than once, "Actions speak louder than words." It's true. Words can be misleading.

If you don't pay attention to the nuances, you'll always be caught off guard by someone's refusal to support your goals and changes. To help you pay attention to the small and telling details you might be missing, keep these facts in mind:

• 65 to 80 percent of communication is nonverbal.

• 50 to 65 percent of one-to-one communication is lost in the first ten minutes.

• We speak at 200 words per minute — and think at **four** times that speed.

• 15 percent of the brain is in use — and the other 85 percent is on vacation.

Our saturation by the media also has an impact on the way we perceive — or fail to perceive — the nuances. Everyone seems to be thinking and speaking in sound bites these days. And too often those conversational snatches are invested with more relevance than they deserve. Misinformation and lies go down easily in the form of bright little bursts of words.

You may know these things, but have forgotten to consider them in your daily collaborations. Keep in mind the following points:

• It is good to make your most important points in 90 seconds of sound bites, but make them substantive and specific. Don't throw out cliches or half-truths. If you need more time to be insightful and to present complex issues, take it, but only after tightly organizing your thoughts. Then make sure the other people participate so they stay involved in the discussion.

• If you know people are shy, lead them gently rather than overwhelming them. Even if you think their comments are mistaken, listen carefully. Just your act of listening will help enlist their collaboration and perhaps improve their thinking.

• Recognizing that you have depended upon the media for your thoughts, ideas, and opinions may encourage you to become a more critical thinker once again — and to formulate your own thoughts, ideas, and opinions.

• Remembering that most people "forget" what is said within minutes may encourage you to write it down, put it in E-mail, or send a reminder note or fax.

• You may be a fast talker, but people think at a greater speed than anyone can talk — and you may not have their full attention. In fact, you may only have a fraction of the brain power most of us use. It's difficult to collaborate when you don't have the other person's attention. Be alert to the nuances indicating you've lost your audience — glazed eyes, fixed smiles, heavy lids, doodling, among others.

What are the major challenges to transformation?

Arrogance. We all have the capacity for arrogance. When you've learned to do something better than most people can do it, you feel justifiably proud. But, if you don't periodically check that nice feeling of satisfaction, it can swell into something less pleasant — like arrogance.

You won't continue to grow in resiliency — to bounce back faster, stronger, and smarter — *if* you give in to arrogance. *If* you stop listening to other's points of view because you think you now have all the answers. *If* you become wedded to the notion of your own rightness.

Transformation is not a state of perfection. It is, by today's criteria, a condition of openness to continuous improvement that is rather humble. Nor will it permit you to assume that your solution to the problem will necessarily be the best one. More businesses fail because the partners' personal attitudes prevented collaboration than fail because of their incompetence.

Failure to make mid-course corrections. Part of a successful corporate turnaround is the mid-course correction. Effective leadership measures progress and reassesses goals — and often leads to revision of the original plan. Apply that practice to both the personal and professional areas of your life. Don't be afraid to stop and turn around.

Failure to reassess can lead people to ignore signs of regression when they occur. Maybe you and your partner are working to improve your relationship. She has agreed to stop criticizing you in public. Then she suddenly reverts to the old habit and dresses you down in front of friends. If you don't confront the behavior but ignore it, hoping it will pass, you can be sure it *will* happen again.

Don't expect recent changes and adaptations to remain stable or fixed for long. You must keep redefining. Remember, transformation is a different attitude toward change and conflict, not a condition in which there is no more change and conflict.

Impatience. You may feel that you "got it." And your improved habits of resiliency are pretty solidly ingrained. You *want* change — and you want it immediately. Forgetting about collaborative respect for others' agendas, you begin to pressure and overreact. You'll get in your own way if you let impatience rule your behavior.

Whether you're attempting change on your job or in your marriage, don't underestimate the time required for transformation. If you're going to make change "second nature," you have to keep working at it every day.

Hanging on. You've changed, so you can't be affected in the old ways by the old people, Wrong! You can't keep one foot in the new and the other in the old. When relationships or partnerships don't work, let go of them. Limit your access to the old people, tasks, habits — and find new ways to reinforce and support the changes you have made.

Be smart about the relationships you can't completely eliminate. You can limit access by ex-spouses, impossible relatives or business associates. For example, if your ex, parent, friend or boss is an alcoholic, see him before he starts drinking at noon.

Don't try to plateau too soon the changes you have made. You may slide back into old habits if you do.

Paul Kaiser began psychotherapy because his marriage was falling apart. The therapist helped him see that the problem was his heavy travel schedule. He returned from frequent and tiring trips feeling angry and impatient with his wife who had adapted to his absence. She resented both his absences and his expectation that she would revert to scheduling her activities around him when he returned.

Paul agreed to eliminate all trips lasting longer than three days. His marriage improved. Within eight months, he felt everything was going so well that he could increase his trips. Within six weeks, his marriage was in trouble again and he was back in the therapist's office.

Letting your guard down — or backsliding - is bound to happen occasionally. You may find yourself relaxing back into old habits. Catch yourself before you fall back too far. Before you take back some of your favorite old habits, such as drinking, avoiding exercising or criticizing others, remind yourself that they did not work for you before. Why would they now?

Consolidating change — good resiliency habits — doesn't come naturally or easily. People who have learned to bounce back faster, stronger and smarter come to enjoy most of the things they gained through effort.

CHAPTER THIRTEEN

BOUNCING BACK
STEP BY STEP:
THE SERIOUS STUFF OF LIFE

***

Besima and Zoran Bozic are a young couple who came to the United States from war-torn Bosnia. A successful economist when war broke out, he was forced to join the Army, was captured and placed in a concentration camp. She didn't know if he was dead or alive until eventually the Red Cross notified her of his general whereabouts.

With the help of an Italian journalist, Zoran escaped. Besima took their baby and fled to join him in Italy. From there, they were sponsored by a cousin who lives in the U.S. and they arrived here with little more than the clothes they were wearing. In their flight to freedom, they had lost home, family, financial resources — everything but each other and their child.

They are learning English and taking any job, from dishwashing to housecleaning, to pay the rent. They are deciding which educational routes will help them get better jobs and provide some future stability. While they receive some support from a refugee program and have been given a loan by the cousin, they are essentially living a meager life compared to the one they had before the war. Who they were is not who they are.

Besima and Zoran have accepted their overwhelming setback with grace and courage.

What are overwhelming setbacks?

William Styron, author of the powerful novel, *Sophie's Choice*, described people's constant complaints about minutia as the "unearned unhappiness" of life. Someone who thinks that a bad haircut or a soggy pizza crust is a disaster has lost their perspective. There are many levels of setbacks, from a hurtful argument to terminal illness. As we've seen, every setback is a challenge to resiliency. And a slew of little annoying problems can provoke an outburst from the most sanguine person.

We do not mean to belittle anyone's everyday struggles but some setbacks are so overwhelming, they must be treated as a separate category. Who hasn't imagined in a blinding flash of fear the accident that would take a loved one's life or the storm capable of blowing the house down or the diagnosis of terminal cancer or the financial devastation so complete that the eviction notice would be served? And how often have we read that the one greatest fear of single women is ending up a bag lady? Some people experience those catastrophic events the rest of us only glimpse briefly in our nightmares and worst fantasies.

The characteristics of an overwhelming setback are:

• The losses suffered are severe.

• The losses suffered are long-lasting or permanent.

• The reality of the situation creates conditions that are extremely limiting.

• The limitations of the situation are unchangeable and therefore not open to negotiation or bargaining. Nor can they be ignored.

You cannot "think" your way out of a catastrophe. The only recourse is to work through it emotionally, mentally, perhaps physically — and follow that work with radical changes of lifestyle. Catastrophic loss always involves grieving, though some people remain in a state of prolonged shock, unable to cry or show emotion.

Penny Turk, the breast cancer survivor you met earlier, talked about grieving in a speech she made about her recovery. Central to her speech is a poem, "To a Young Girl, Spring and Fall," by Gerard Manley Hopkins. In this poem, Margaret, a young girl, is weeping for the fallen leaves of a tree. The poet tells her that although she will become hardened to the death of leaves in time, she will continue to weep and will finally discover that it is her own mortality that brings her tears.

"It is the blight that man was born for.
It is Margaret you mourn for."

"My name is Penny and I am a cancer survivor," she began. "It took me a long time to learn to say that. It was hard to say the word 'cancer' and in learning to say it, I prove to myself that I am learning to cope with my experience and the memories and scars that it has left behind.

"A friend of mine sent me this poem the day before that first gynecological appointment. The next day I wrote back, 'Yesterday you sent me a poem about Margaret. Today I am Margaret. I have met Margaret and I am she.' The first stage in my coping with cancer was grief, like Margaret I would 'weep and know why.'

"In my second stage of coping, I saw the poem as a comforting reminder that none of us is alone in our trouble. Ours is the human condition, 'the blight that man was born for.' The second stage for me was a stoic acceptance.

"I also very much liked having Margaret as a symbol of my weaker moments and since, those were always when I was alone, I took to talking to Margaret out loud. At one point, I believe I told her that I planned to beat her to death, poor child. I got tough on Margaret. 'Stop sniveling, my girl,' I told her. 'You are acting a little self-centered and ridiculous anyway. All of the unleaving (and leaving) are God's plan and the vast cyclic pattern of nature. Dry your eyes and get back to the business of living. It's one day at a time, so stiffen the backbone and carry on.'

"Finally I made my peace with Margaret...in the necessary acceptance of my situation. The real message of Hopkins' poem is that it is all right to cry. I have earned the tears. I am now into the stage I call endurance, which promises to be a very long stage.

"I have found great help in this stage through the three P's of prayer, people, and prose and poetry. I like talking to God. He is neither shocked nor burdened by the outpouring of my soul."

Penny Turk, with a little help from Margaret, worked through her grief. She attributes her resiliency to a shift in perspective gained through the three P's. With that help, she moved from being an "anticipatory" person to one who lives only one day at a time.

When grief remains unresolved, an effective response to challenge is impossible. More losses often follow and the situation grows worse. This is the downward spiral — and here's how it works:

A 54-year-old man may abruptly lose his job, his career terminated by reorganization or technological changes. The financial and psychological crisis may lead to losing his home. Then his shaky marriage may collapse. Divorce alienates him from his children, in-laws, shared friends and neighbors. The deepening loss of support and security immobilizes him. Perhaps he drinks excessively, has a brief affair that ends badly, and spirals him into further loss. What began as the loss of a job becomes the loss of a life, from which he must now struggle to recover step by step. This man suffered a loss and, by his own actions, turned it into a personal catastrophe.

The types of overwhelming setbacks

The kinds of catastrophic losses include those so fundamental to human survival that anyone who experiences them will be knocked down. The Holocaust, the wars in Bosnia and Rwanda, the terrorist bombing in Oklahoma City — all are examples. No one walks out of a catastrophe unscathed. And what of the young woman trapped in the rubble of the federal building in Oklahoma City whose leg was amputated without anesthesia? She lost not only her leg but her mother and two children in that tragedy.

Other catastrophes are strongly affected by the individual's vulnerabilities to them. They include physical assaults — particularly on children or the elderly — total financial loss — particularly for those too old or too ill to recover — and loss of a person on whom the sufferer is completely dependent. When an elderly couple have only each other and one dies, the other is often resigned to just surviving, without sufficient time to build a new life.

Sometimes vulnerability is created by repeated personal losses occurring rapidly within a brief period of time.

Sherry Hill Sexton is an intrepid entrepreneur — and was from early childhood. Born in Iowa, an only child, she created her own garden and seed catalogue when she was eight. At fourteen, she began her sales career working in a local department store. When she was

141

eighteen, she pulled up in the front of her house in her own car and told her mother that she was moving to California. Her mother went along — leaving her work, friends, and established life to support her daughter's dreams. Today Sherry is the president of Celebrity Properties, a Beverly Hills real estate business which she started part-time while still a hair stylist for the film industry.

The darkest year of Sherry's life coincided with the worst real estate depression in California since the Great Depression in the thirties. She worked hard to motivate her agents and hit the road every day herself making cold calls to list low-end houses. Then her beloved mother died. Her dog died. And her marriage fell apart.

She says, "I had a bout with cancer, too, but that was nothing, compared to the loss of my mother, my dog, my marriage and the renting of my dream home in the course of one year."

Sherry moved in with a woman friend, lived on her credit cards, and rebuilt her business step by step.

Finally, there is a more individualized form of catastrophe which may not look like a catastrophe at all to others. The person loses something of enormous value to his sense of identity. A priest may lose his faith in God. A man who has nothing in his life but his job may lose it and feel he has lost himself. A woman whose life is her children may feel absolutely without personal identity if they move far away.

Without a strong sense of their own worth, people are fragile. In *Man's Search For Meaning*, Viktor Frankl reported that the first deaths in concentration camps were among those individuals who had no sense of their own value outside their status in the community. Removed from the community and thrown into the camps, they succumbed rapidly.

Coming back from overwhelming setbacks

Before Ruth Finley was thirty, she had lost her father to a heart attack, and her beloved 29-year-old brother to cancer. A few years later, her husband died from a heart attack as he was walking out of his doctor's office, leaving her with three boys under ten years of age. Ruth was a widow before she was 35.

"His death was such a horrible shock," she says. "I remember being at the morgue with a friend. Nothing seemed real. For two weeks after the funeral, I kept asking myself, 'How am I going to do this alone?' I had no confidence in myself."

Despite the shock, she began to plan and strategize. She asked herself, "How can I handle this catastrophe?" She began to pick up the pieces, with the help of her friends and her work, because her children needed her.

"I became determined that life would go on for them, that they would take vacations as they had before, that I would be the den mother for cub scouts, and take them to games. We would continue to eat in our favorite restaurants."

Ruth had run her own business for several years and opted to continue self-employment because she wanted to remain close to home for her children. Though she experienced her share of difficulties — including neighborhood mothers worrying that their husbands might find the young widow attractive — she raised her sons and turned her small business of coordinating the fashion industry's shows into a huge success.

How did she pull herself out of the grief which engulfed her after her husband's death?

"It was *necessary*, therefore it was possible," she says. "Thank God for my kids. I was so lucky to have those three boys who needed me."

Ruth Finley didn't go into a downward spiral, but many people do. Perhaps you are in one now.

How to stop a downward spiral

As soon as you sense you are cascading downward, you must do something constructive to halt the spiral. Access the energy in your anger and fear and put it to positive use. If you are ill, begin medical treatment immediately. If you have no insurance or resources, apply for help and contact anyone you know who might intervene in your behalf. If you are facing litigation or financial moves against you, find a lawyer, including low-fee or advocate legal services. If you can't stop shaking or crying long enough to engage personal support systems, find a professional counselor or psychotherapist, including low-cost services. Contact any friend or family member who might help.

We have developed the following exercise to help you see the possibilities when you are feeling overwhelmed.

EXERCISE: *The cascading system for problem solving*

When faced with overwhelming setbacks, you may understandably see only the negatives in a situation. This will help you find the positives — and show you how you can "cascade" your options by looking at a negative and a positive for every negative.

1. Look at the problem.

2. Write down two positives and two negatives.

3. Now write one negative and one positive for each of those positives and negatives.

4. Continue doing this — cascading the negatives and positives — until you have **exhausted all possibilities** for looking at the situation differently. You will be amazed at the positives you find. For every negative, there is truly a *possibility*.

Catastrophic physical illness

Sometimes the catastrophe has invaded your own body. There is no place to run or hide. You have to fight in place.

Edward Stautberg is only 11, but he takes nine to thirteen pills a day to treat his Crohn's disease, a painful disorder of the intestinal tract. This regimen will continue for the rest of his life. His remarkable and resilient mother refuses to "smother" him. She lets him do all the things other children do, like soccer, and has taken him on

THE CASCADING SYSTEM FOR PROBLEM SOLVING

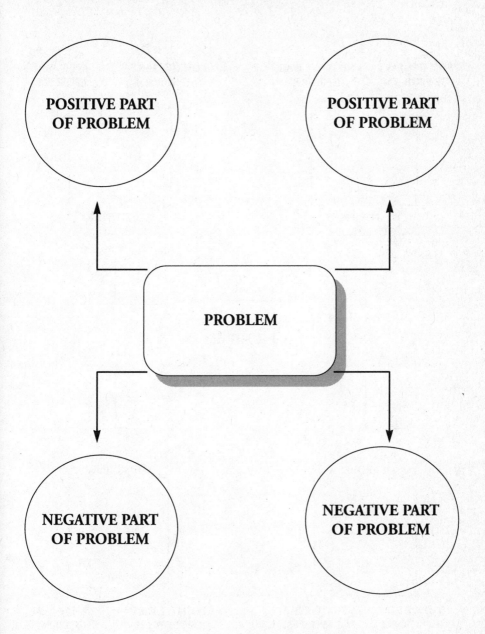

THE CASCADING SYSTEM FOR PROBLEM SOLVING

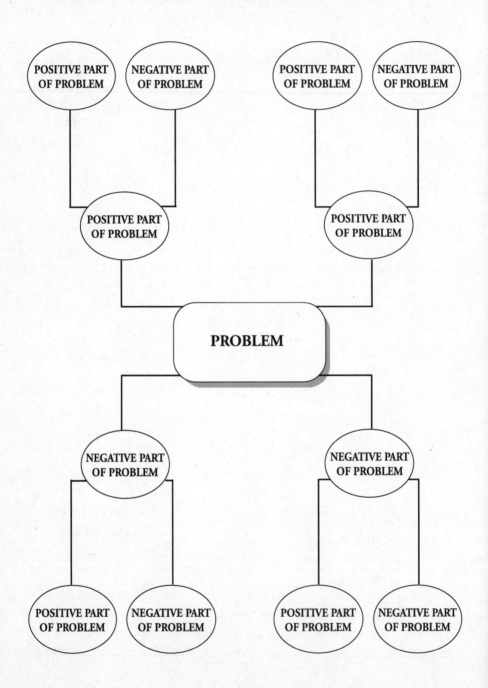

"adventures," including a trip to the Andes.

"I don't make a big deal out of it," Edward says of his disease, which had initially left him afraid to eat because of the pain that can occur.

Josh Friedman's cancer had been in remission for fourteen years when his doctor told him he had prostate cancer. He and his wife were determined that he would come through this crisis, too.

The family carefully strategized his recovery, taking the following steps:

1. They researched the literature thoroughly.
2. They interviewed physicians about their procedures.
3. They talked to other recovering patients.
4. They revamped the family diet by working with a nutritionist.
5. Josh meditated twice daily for weeks before hospitalization.
6. They listened daily to relaxation and self-enhancement tapes in the hospital and when Josh returned home.
7. They called on their community and friends for visits and encouragement.
8. Josh disciplined his activities to increase daily, walking one-fourth block for three days, then one-half block. As his stamina increased, he played golf and hand ball regularly.
9. Josh took the recovery period as an opportunity to plan his next career.

This kind of recovery takes work. The Friedman family declared war on Josh's cancer and so far they are winning. Retired from a 30-year career in the educational system. Josh has now begun a private practice to guide and counsel seniors in career transitions.

Alcoholism is also a catastrophic illness for many people.

Charlotte Bridges, a 52-year-old mother of three, kept her drinking under control while she lived a storybook life in Europe as the wife of a successful man. Following the divorce and her return to the U. S., she began drinking heavily. Seeing the pain she was causing her family written in her son's face, she admitted herself to a residential treatment program. After twelve years, she had a relapse, which she considers her "turning point."

"I cannot drink if I want to be in this world," she says. "After the relapse, I made a true commitment to myself. I made the choice not to drink for me."

This type of recovery takes work. *You* have to make a choice to do the work. Once you have made that choice, break the work down into stages.

1. Don't run away from the problem.

You need to have a clear head now. People who deal with trauma by relying on alcohol, drugs, food, shopping, gambling, or other addictions are running away by hurling themselves into a mental fog. And, when you're severely distressed, even two glasses of wine can have a stronger impact on you than they normally would, because body chemistry is radically altered in a traumatic situation.

2. Form a plan for stability.

Get support and practical feedback from professionals or trusted family and friends. Then create a plan to stabilize your disrupted life. If it involves financial disaster, for example, a temporary or permanent lifestyle change may be necessary. Reduce your overhead by renting or selling your residence and moving somewhere cheaper. Cut up the credit cards. Get a roommate. People can downsize just as companies do.

3. Find a safe space.

Finding a safe physical space where you can recover and think is a priority. That space may be inside your own home or the hour a week you spend in a therapist's office or a park bench or a shelter for refugees from domestic violence. We saw a news story last year about a 79-year-old woman who had lost her job and her home following a small stroke. She put all of her belongings in a self-storage unit and was living next to it in her car. In addition to desperation, she may have had some hope that a solution would come and, in the meantime, she found temporary stability in a safe place — her car.

Coming up from the bottom

Sarah Osborne, a beautiful and intense 43-year-old woman given to drama in her personal life, almost let a failed relationship destroy her body. She had been living with a man for over ten years when it finally became clear to both of them that "things were no longer working out." Rather than accepting a break at that point, she tried to hold on.

Though she has ulcerative colitis that requires she be vigilant about her eating, sleeping and exercise habits, she stopped taking care of her health. For eight months she was very ill.

"I looked anorexic when I finally hit bottom and was willing to give up the relationship," she says. "I agreed that he would have to move out, which he had been wanting to do. I'd kept him with me out of guilt. How could he leave me when I was so sick?"

Osborne tapped into the resiliency inside her. She went back to her good health habits, including exercise, reconnected with old friends, and slowly began working again. She also did something to help her bounce back from her overwhelming setback more quickly: She took a risk a day to get her self-confidence back.

The following exercise will teach you how to do that, too. But, we caution that taking a risk a day might be too much for someone with less natural resiliency than Osborne has. She was able to use the technique as her springboard. You might want to wait until you are stronger — or modify it to a risk every other day or every week or take small risks, such as walking a different path, trying a new food.

EXERCISE: Risk-a-day

A risk a day builds resiliency.

1. **Join the risk takers.** Make a list of the risk takers you know. Call at least one of them every day. Arrange to have lunch or coffee with them if you can. Ask them about the risks they have taken in life.

2. **Stay focused.** Rather than making scattered risks, let your risks build on one another. Have a goal in mind.

3. Trust yourself. You can't take risks if you don't. Each risk increases your self-esteem, which increases your options. In the beginning, you may trust others, especially risk-takers, more than you trust yourself. Their support should help you begin to recover your resiliency.

Life after the downward spiral

Kate Paulson worked for a visible, high-powered corporation — one of those companies that makes the news — but she hated her job. For three years, she didn't do anything about finding a job she would like. Then she had back surgery. Shortly afterward, her boss told her that her position would soon be terminated. While recovering from surgery and working 14-hour days, she had to begin her job search.

Because she loved the California lifestyle, she explored opportunities on the West Coast. By the time she got her pink slip, she'd made the decision to relocate and go into business for herself. It was not an easy move. Her significant love relationship ended because he did not want to move or be part of a long distance love affair. She lost easy access to her extended family. And she sold many of her possessions.

Kate suffered a year of panic attacks, daily anxiety, depression, and sometimes rage. The burglary of her self-storage unit at one point became her proverbial last straw. But her story has a positive outcome. With the help of counseling, she has begun to make a new life, filled with the outdoor activities she loves.

Kate pulled out of her downward spiral — a feat made all the more difficult because, like most people, she couldn't afford the luxury of not making a living while she recovered from loss.

Few people can take a lot of time out in life. It would be lovely if people could always stop, reflect, and then respond. But typically they have to reflect and respond all at once, while they're trying to make the rent money. We call that operating on a dual track. The immediate financial needs must be acknowledged and met while you spend your spare moments working on the long-term goals.

To put yourself on the dual track, you must:

Inventory your resources. Within a temporary or enduring safe space, take an inventory of your resources. They may include:

-Personal assets. Your resiliency is an asset! Others are good health, available time, education, talents you can further develop, life and work skills. Imagine your "resume": good with people; 32 years of experience in organizations; computer competency; 20 years as a good parent/homemaking executive.

-Interpersonal assets. Extended family and friends, clubs, associations and organizations designed to help with your particular problem, self-support groups, professional associates, old mentors.

-Physical resources. Your home, office, savings, investments, property, physical health, libraries, local colleges or universities, senior centers, books, computers, etc.

Form a strategy for recovery that has structure and flexibility. Examine your resources. What does the list tell you?

Ask yourself some specific questions. If you have stabilized your situation, is the status quo good enough? If the answer is, "No", you need a plan that is larger than the immediate situation. But the plan should be realistic, based on actual resources or ones that are likely within reach.

How long will it take to mobilize your resources to implement a new plan? Remember that the further you are into the hole, the higher you must leap to bounce back. Big leaps take time.

Beginning a new chapter

If you are beginning a new chapter, you are not alone.

Millions of Americans lose their jobs every year. And millions *hate* their jobs and suffer from the stress that creates. They would love to begin a new chapter, if only they knew how. Others are relocated, either by choice or necessity. The average American will move eleven times in a lifetime. And the average lifetime of the largest industrial enterprises is less than forty years. We are a nation of movers, of companies starting up and going under, of people starting over.

Another way people start over is through divorce. Some remarry and start new, or blended, families. And often women are left to raise children alone in greatly reduced circumstances. The number of women having babies outside marriage has also increased. The proportion of American children growing up in homes without a father had quadrupled since 1950 to 24 percent, or 19 million, in 1994.

Finally, some people are beginning new lives as cancer survivors, widows or widowers, or survivors of other catastrophes. As Gail Sheehy, author of *New Passages*, says, "Resilience is probably the most important protection one can have. People who have met and mastered most of the passages and predictable crises of life up to now are, by definition, resilient." We can't suggest pragmatic solutions for all the problems overwhelming people today. But we can tell you how to use your resiliency to build a new life.

The love core

Love is the core of a new start.

Now that you have stabilized your position — even if the position is at or near the bottom — and have taken an inventory of resources and developed a strategy, we strongly urge you to focus on a core issue which excites your passion. In our experience as psychotherapists and teachers, we have seen that the best predictor of success in any enterprise is passion. If you love what you are doing, you are far more likely to succeed.

Bouncing back from the bottom step-by-step can be very slow and is likely to be difficult, too. Love will make all the difference. If you commit to someone or something, to a plan, a job, a move that you do not love — you will be discouraged at the first serious setback.

Search for what you love. If the word "love" makes you nervous, search for what you really like or enjoy the most in life. Search for what makes you feel good. We know that the longest and most tortuous struggle people experience is not in surmounting the obstacles to profound change but in searching for what they really love and want. Joseph Campbell's most famous line in *The Power of Myth* was: "Follow your bliss." Not a simple path to follow, but possible.

Sometimes you have to search back into your memories of the past, all the way back to your childhood or youth. Manny Vitelli was feeling stuck in his career as an investment counselor for years before he came to a "breakthrough" in his personal therapy. During several probing sessions about his interests in adolescence, he recalled his great passion for discos and dancing, which he dropped as his career took off. Following the emotional high he felt from that memory, he began to explore a partnership investment in a struggling, but promising, club in the city. His career continued for another few years while he developed a string of partnerships in several discos, but then his "adolescent passion" became his second career.

Sometimes the answers aren't in the past but in the present — in the people and places, friends and activities, and hobbies you love. Like Bill Strickler, who developed his second career out of his love of birds and wildlife, you may find your new beginning where you would never have thought to look before.

And sometimes the answers aren't in the past or present, but in the search itself. Did you ever find something you thought was long lost while looking for something else? A search for your glasses turns up a missing earring, for example. Similarly, your search could lead you to discover something you didn't even know was missing or hadn't ever realized you liked.

Dr. Barlow had a client who could not find what she wanted or loved. She had endured two difficult job experiences while devoting herself to caring for her father following the death of her mother. When her father and her beloved dog died within a month of each other, she had no idea what to do with her time. She kept worrying about her "career," but she had absolutely no feeling for any of her previous interests.

Finally Dr. Barlow asked her, "What would you most like to do when you wake up tomorrow if you didn't have to think about your career?"

Without hesitation, she replied, "Take my new puppy to the beach for the day."

She did take her puppy to the beach the next day and again the following day. The walk on the beach became a habit. As she walked, she began thinking about beachfront enterprises and talking to people she met about jobs and apartments near the beach. She is still engaged in her search for her passion — but she is actively enjoying the search now.

Love is the core of a new start *and* of resiliency. You cannot make an unambivalent commitment to life without passion.

What if you have no passion?

We aren't pretending this is an original piece of advice. For thousands of years, people have been telling each other, "When you are at the bottom, look around for someone worse off than you and count your blessings." We only add: Give what you have to this person who has less.

How can you give if you have nothing to give?

You can give hope and comfort and encouragement. In giving courage, you find it in yourself. In giving hope and imagination, you are inspired. When you give, you receive. And suddenly your own empty places begin to fill.

Where does resiliency really come from if not inside you?

Betsy Kleeblatt is recognized by many people who visit Washington, D.C., as the special event planner who arranged and organized their group tour in the city. However, many people in Washington know her in an entirely different role as the co-leader, with her husband, of The Compassionate Friends, the Washington-Bethesda chapter of a national volunteer self-help organization to provide support and counseling for people who have suffered the death of one or more of their children.

It was almost eight years ago when Betsy's eldest son Jamie, thirteen years old at the time, was killed in a farming accident. He died of cardiac arrest on the Medivac airlift.

In recounting that painful period, Betsy remembers that she and her husband quickly turned to caring for their two living sons, eight and 11. This concern for the welfare of the boys became a primary source of strength throughout the period following the tragedy.

The support from their large community of friends was another source of resiliency that was vital to the family. Over 600 people came to share their grief at a memorial service. Even so, Betsy says, "The single best piece of advice received back then was from my uncle, who had lost a daughter to Hodgkins disease. He told me that you never get over the death of a child: you just get used to living with it."

Betsy has shared that and other helpful insights with many people in the past eight years through her involvement with The Compassionate Friends. She and her husband began to attend group meetings a few months after Jamie's death. "The reason I want to continue with the group," says Betsy, "is because it really helps people. There are others who have been involved for years who gave me the hope that I try to pass on to others."

And what are some of the observations that can be helpful?

1. Common belief has it that the death of a child is destructive to most marriages, but Betsy insists that is not her experience. In many families, the husband and wife are equally involved in the process of recovery and marriages often grow closer. She believes, however, that men and women express their grief somewhat differently and each can experience hurt when the other spouse doesn't appear to feel the same things they do.

2. Organ donation can be extremely healing. In the act of helping others whose lives can be saved or enhanced, the death of a loved one assumes greater meaning and purpose.

3. "I always believed that life is 10 percent what happens to you and 90 percent how you react to it," says Betsy. "There are always choices to be made. You can choose to collapse or you can choose to go

forward. Giving in to self-pity is utterly destructive to resiliency. You can't pull yourself up if you're thinking about yourself and your pain."

4. Betsy believes that there is nothing worse than the loss of a child. For her and for many others, the question becomes: "After this, what else is there to be afraid of?" There's hope when your perspective grows larger regarding what you believe you can handle.

PART FIVE

THE SPIRITUAL CONNECTION

CHAPTER FOURTEEN

THE RESPONSIBILITY OF CHOOSING

Janet Bell traces the loss of resiliency — which she didn't regain for many years — to an important moment when she was five or six. On a wooden platform in a willow tree overlooking the lake, she frequently talked to God. Then huge spiders moved into the space.

"I vividly remember my inner dialogue," she says. "I asked, ' Do I love God more or do I fear the spiders more?' The spiders won! I think I terminated my relationship with God at that point."

Janet Bell is now a resilient, agile, intelligent woman of 81 years. The death of her husband when she was 54 left her bereft. She transferred her dependency to her sister — which enabled her to extend her patterns of coping by relying on someone else for years. When her sister became seriously ill and had to be placed in a nursing home, Janet went into a downward spiral. Through the help of her daughter and friends in a support group, she began to bounce back.

Now, she says, "I have concluded that some of the worst things that have happened, like the death of my husband and the collapse of my sister, have also brought me some of the best things of my life: a degree of independent functioning, and better ability to take charge of my life, to stay in the present, and to reduce catastrophic thinking. My mantra is: This is a fine, pain-free, worry-free moment in which there is nothing to fear. Enjoy it.

"I am still fear-based but I am better. A brilliant friend taught me that fear is twofold: lack of faith and lack of experience. I now have plenty of faith but experience is hard to come by when you're terrified to change and risk. But I continue to work on this and I see improvement.

"I changed my attitude. I know that I am fully responsible for myself and my behavior. I'm not into the kind of helplessness I suffered from all my life. I've learned absolutely that I have choices, especially over my attitude. No matter how catastrophic a thing is, there are ways to deal with it. I'm not hopeless anymore.

"I have come to believe that there is a cosmic connection linked to something in me that is working for my survival and well-being. I can't say I've had a spiritual experience of the sort that some people describe — nothing mystical, really.

"But I heard someone describe a spiritual experience as 'a character change sufficient to overcome compulsion.' I've had that. I'm not that other person now."

The spiritual connection is the link between the "cosmic" and you. People who believe in God sometimes call the link "the God within." Others refer to their spiritual side as their "real self," "inner voice," or "the still, small voice." Whatever term you use to describe it, this spiritual connection to the universe, God, or simply other people — something beyond ourselves - defines us as human beings.

How important is the spiritual connection to resiliency?

We believe it is almost impossible to have an unambivalent commitment to life — the basis of resiliency — without a spiritual connection.

In recent years many Americans have become increasingly concerned with developing their spirituality. They are on a serious search for real meaning in their lives. A recent *Newsweek* poll showed 58 percent of Americans say they feel the need to experience spiritual growth.

Why at this point in our history are so many people hungry for that meaning? Many social commentators cite the aging of the Baby Boom generation as a causative factor. Certainly, there is some truth in this. As people reach middle age, they do begin to look around and ask themselves, "Isn't there more to my life than this struggle for material things? Is that all there is?"

But we have seen in our practices and our work with executives that the spiritual hunger goes beyond the Boomers and reaches into the hearts of younger and older people, too. We believe it is tied to the increasing need for resiliency. As the speed of change increases and the need for resiliency grows, so does the need for the spiritual connection.

Samuel Brown, cantor emeritus of Temple Beth Hillel, Valley

Village, California, says, "Personal spirituality is about coming to grips with life itself. We are all subject to the same rules as all other living things. We are born and we die."

The last verse from the credo (hymn), "The God of All" expresses it best:

> *Into God's hands, I entrust my spirit,*
> *When I sleep and when I wake*
> *And with my spirit, my body also;*
> *God is with me, I will not fear.*

"This last verse has always filled me with strength and comfort," Sam says. "I sing or recite it with firm belief."

Perhaps the speed of change we now experience has made that simple truth all the more obvious to anyone who is paying attention.

How can you use the tools of resiliency building to develop spirituality?

Viktor Frankl's basic belief is that man's ultimate freedom is choosing the position and the attitude he takes toward his situation. We also share that belief. Choosing is central to building resiliency and developing spirituality, and learning to choose has been a focus of this book. In chapters devoted to perspective, authenticity and conscience, imagination and hope, and negotiating and collaboration — we have tried to help you see how to make choices that nurture these conditions of resiliency. If you make the choices that help you grow in resiliency, you cannot help but develop a deeper sense of spirituality, in whatever way you define or express it.

The late Miriam Teel Clarke, once explained the core of her spiritual beliefs in this way: "In the act of choosing, we are closest to God, because we are assuming personal responsibility to participate in the cosmic evolution. At least in that part of it that is human and therefore within our reach."

To act from your God within — or to be true to your inner self

161

- you must choose to act with integrity and authenticity. Ultimately, the commitment to life that is resiliency is expressed in the thousands of life-affirming choices resilient people make each day.

Elie Wiesel — holocaust survivor, author, playwright, journalist and lecturer — has written eloquently about both the horrors of the concentration camps and the strength of the human spirit. To quote phrases of his work is almost to do him an injustice. The scope of his great moral stature and writing talent cannot be captured in a few lines. We cannot resist, however, repeating these beautiful words about choice:

"God requires of man not that he live, but that he choose to live. What matters is to choose — at the risk of being defeated."

Throughout this book, we have stated our belief that resiliency is, in its essence, an unambivalent commitment to life. Humankind has been concerned forever with an effort to define the most important and fundamental commitment of each era.

Out of the church came the affirmation, "I believe, therefore I am." Out of the age of reason came, "I think, therefore I am." Out of the Industrial Revolution came, "I work, therefore I am."

At the end of the industrial age in the twentieth century, we are engaged in a renewed effort to define who we are. Thus the spiritual quest for self-definition. That leads us to affirm: I choose, therefore I am.

Choosing to collaborate

We have seen in our work that collaboration is essential to resiliency. Yet, there is nothing more individual than acting from your voice within. Is that a contradiction? People who fear collaboration and commitment often use their individuality as an excuse. "How can I be true to myself and consider someone else?" they ask. We believe that only in being true to your own voice can you collaborate successfully. The authentic self chooses an honest commitment that is not a threat to individuality.

In the last chapter, we talked about finding your passion and living the life you love. When you do that, your spiritual connection to God, or your inner self, and to other people grows stronger. Compassion and respect for other people — and their inner voices — is a fundamental requirement for collaboration. Love of self and respect for others goes hand in hand.

Resiliency requires a commitment to all three dimensions: the universal or cosmic, the self and the human community. Former cabinet secretary John Gardner, the 82-year-old founder of both the White House Fellowships and Common Cause, recently launched The Alliance for National Renewal, a consortium of more than 90 groups dedicated to community problem solving. His vision of renewal is compatible with our definition of resiliency.

"People want meaning in their lives; but in this turbulent era a context of meaning is rarely handed to us as a comfortable inheritance. Today we have to build meaning into our lives, and we build it through our commitments — to our religion, our conception of an ethical order, to our loved ones, to our community, to unborn generations," he said in a recent speech. "One such commitment is service to one's community."

All of the people who appear in this book have reported that their journeys back from losses and setbacks to renewal, recovery and resiliency have involved turning their private pain over to something or someone beyond themselves. Turning to God, a "cosmic something," their families, friends or their communities was the source of renewed energy, solace and strength. The recovery of inner resources and their sense of self - the inner voice declaring, "I can do it!" — activated the heart and soul of their resiliency.

Making the leap of faith

Faith is often called a leap. We find that appropriate. Resiliency requires a lot of faith and leaping.

"How else could you possibly move from one point to another when there is no direct link?" asks Robert Schuller. "Faith is leaping across gaps that exist between the known and the unknown, the proven and the unproven, the actual and the possible, the grasp and the reach...By a running leap, I will jump into tomorrow with expectancy! There is always a chasm between my present achievement and my unfulfilled hopes and dreams. By faith I make the leap and grow. "

We heard so many wonderful stories of spirituality and resiliency while working on this book. One of those was Bobbie Jordan's. You met her in an earlier chapter where she described her childhood, which was heavily influenced by her mother and her aunts. In 1989 she was diagnosed with breast cancer and had a mastectomy followed by chemotherapy. That experience strengthened her resiliency and deepened and expanded her spirituality.

"The person who put me in touch with my spirit at this time was a woman," she says, "an educator, a therapist and specialist in death and dying, a native American of Cherokee heritage, and a good personal friend."

"After the first chemo treatment, I went to her and said, 'Help. I'm never going to get through this by myself. What can you do to help me?' She prescribed a daily program of meditation exercises first. I had learned to successfully meditate a few years back, but was rusty. Then she brought out her Indian Medicine cards, spread them on the table, and asked me to 'pick a card.' My hand hesitated a moment and then landed on the Elk. I will never forget the message until the day I die. It essentially said: The Elk is a long-distance runner. He cannot outrun his enemy, the wolf, through speed, so he does it by endurance. He simply keeps his eyes on the sun, and paces himself until he leaves all of his dangers behind.

"A later session with my friend gave me the Coyote for humor — a major healing weapon that I had lost along the way, and several other spiritual partners for my perilous journey.

"I wish I could say I had an epiphany when lightning flashed and it all came together. But, I did not. My spiritual healing was as slow and arduous as my physical healing.

"I began to chant up the sun every day: to allow the rays of goodness and power to enter my body; to ask for the strength to be a light to others; to feel connected to every part of the universe and to recognize my place in it. My world shifted from a Bobbie-centered universe to a world of infinite possibilities.

"There is this fierce and powerful spirit inside me now. Perhaps it has always been here, but it took a huge catastrophe to bring it center stage. I have a fantastic *joie de vivre*. I cherish every day. I hold on to all of the good energy that comes my way, and I let go of the negative demons."

Joie de vivre

We share a heartfelt prayer that not one of you finishes this book, lays it down, and goes on as you were before. In our work with people, we have the — sometimes happy, sometimes sad — opportunity to see men and women every day who are struggling to optimize their lives in the face of extreme challenges. Most of the time, the challenges are not serious external problems but the mental and emotional problem of loss of resiliency — burnout. Loss of passion and interest, accompanied by confusion about goals and values, manifest every day in millions of people. Only through the courage it takes to look honestly at yourself and your life, with another person for feedback and support, do people achieve transformation and reenter the game of life reenergized and feeling good again.

There is no doubt that the future is uncertain and demanding as we enter the twenty-first century. What will it take to handle it with resiliency? Like Bobbie Jordan, it will require "this fierce and powerful spirit inside!" You need *joie de vivre,* anchored in a perspective that protects your core values, beliefs, and deepest loves and wishes. You need an unambivalent commitment to life.

The late Maggie Kuhn, founder of the Gray Panthers, an international group committed to defend the rights and needs of the elderly, was an intrepid, outspoken individualist who never backed down from anything or anyone. Her resiliency throughout a life of adventure and achievement is legendary.

She once said she wanted this line carved on her tombstone:

"Here lies Maggie Kuhn under the only stone she left unturned."

If you wish to ensure your own resiliency now and in the future, make choices every day that renew this spiritual connection. You might begin today. ✳

ABOUT THE AUTHORS

Tessa Albert Warschaw, Ph.D. a distinguished psychotherapist and nationally known specialist in personal and corporate negotiation strategies, wrote the pioneering *Winning by Negotiation*. She's also authored the groundbreaking book *Rich is Better: How Women Can Bridge the Gap Between Wanting and Having It All* and co-authored *Winning with Kids.*

Warschaw maintains private therapy practices in New York and Los Angeles, and is president of the Warschaw Group, a private group of business consultants and work-family counselors. A compelling motivational speaker, she has appeared on the *The Today Show, Oprah Winfrey, Live with Regis and Kathy Lee, Good Morning Washington,* and *A.M. Los Angeles.*

Dee Barlow, Ph.D., provides psychotherapy and consultaion to individuals and dual-career couples in Beverly Hills. Her work with senior creative executives and artists in the entertainment industry led to a particular interest in resiliency in highly productive professionals.

Barlow was a professor at the University of New South Wales in Sydney, Australia and at the California Institute for Clinical Social Work. She was a major contributor to the best-selling book, *Mirages of Marriage.*

MASTERMEDIA LIMITED

To order copies of Resiliency: How to Bounce Back Faster, Stronger, Smarter ($21.95) hardbound, send a check for the price of each book ordered plus $2 postage and handling for the first book, and $1 for each additional copy to:

MasterMedia Limited
17 East 89th Street
New York, NY 10128
(212) 260-5600
(800) 334-8232 *please use MasterCard or VISA on phone orders*
(212) 546-7638 (fax)

AN INVITATION

If you found this book helpful, you may want to receive an inspirational newsletter from **The Heritage Imprint**, a list of inspirational books from MasterMedia, the only company to combine publishing with a full service speakers bureau.

MasterMedia books and speakers cover today's important issues, from family values to health topics and business ethics.

For the Heritage Newsletter or a MasterMedia book catalog, write or fax to the above address or phone number.

For information and a complete list of speakers, call (800) 453-2887 or fax (908) 359-1647

RESILIENCY SEMINARS:
HOW TO BOUNCE BACK FASTER, STRONGER, SMARTER

This seminar includes lively, interactive exercises that allows participants to take a paper and pencil to their lives in order to bounce back from life's challenges, personally and professionally - from a bad day to a bad marriage, verbal insult to physical trauma, loss of a job to loss of a business, a boss who makes every minute difficult to a tragic accident that in a split second changes your future forever.

Surviving such destabilization is not enough. We must recover. We must make up our minds to leap over obstacles and take control of our lives again. We must have the courage to ask ourselves:

- How equipped am I to deal with the next challenge life may throw at me?
- What is my resiliency quotient?
- Can I raise my resiliency quotient?
- Am I a survivor or a person with resiliency?

Participants will learn the answer to these questions and about:

- Recognizing, understanding and increasing the components of resiliency
- Moving through the three stages of resiliency- holding on, letting go, moving on
- Developing the skills to move faster, be stronger, strategize smarter.

Program length: 3 hours Interactive seminar; 1 hour Keynote

For more information, call Tony Calao, director of MasterMedia's Speakers' Bureau at 800-453-2887.

SEMINARS FOR THE SERIOUS NEGOTIATOR.

Presented by Dr. Tessa Albert Warschaw, contact Tony Calao, Director of MasterMedia's Speakers' Bureau at 800-453-2887

- Negotiating in the 21st Century: The Age of Collaboration
- Negotiating from "A-to-Z" in an Atmosphere of Change
- Negotiating with Adversarial Partners, Colleagues, Customers and Clients
- Corporate Conflicts: Recognizing, Understanding, Predicting and Resolving
- Managerial Strategies for Building a Team that Creates, Works and Thinks About the Bottom Line.
- Igniting Creativity - Accessing Untapped Potential
- Collaborators that Work, Play and Make Money Together
- Rich is Better: How Women Can Bridge the Gap from Wanting to Have It All - Financiall, Emotionally, Professionally
- Making the Shift from a Corporate to Entrepreneurial Spirit

OTHER MASTERMEDIA BOOKS

To order additional copies of any MasterMedia book, send a check for the price of the book plus $2.00 postage and handling for the first book, $1.00 for each additional book to:

MasterMedia Limited
17 East 89th Street
New York, NY 10128
(212) 260-5600
(800) 334-8232 please use MasterCard or VISA on phone orders
(212) 546-7638 (fax)

AGING PARENTS AND YOU: A Complete Handbook to Help You Help Your Elders Maintain a Healthy, Productive and Independent Life, by Eugenia Anderson-Ellis, is a complete guide to providing care to aging relatives. It gives practical advice and resources to adults who are helping their elders lead productive and independent lives. Revised and updated. ($9.95 paper)

BALANCING ACTS! Juggling Love, Work, Family, and Recreation, by Susan Schiffer Stautberg and Marcia L. Worthing, provides strategies to achieve a balanced life by reordering priorities and setting realistic goals. ($12.95 paper)

BOUNCING BACK: How to Turn Business Crises Into Success, by Harvey Reese. Based on interviews with entrepreneurs from coast to coast, this fascinating book contains cautionary tales that unfold with gripping suspense. Reese has discovered a formula for success that should be "must reading" for every new or budding entrepreneur. ($18.95 hardbound)

BREATHING SPACE: Living and Working at a Comfortable Pace in a Sped-Up Society, by Jeff Davidson, helps readers to handle information and activity overload and gain greater control over their lives. ($10.95 paper)

CITIES OF OPPORTUNITY: Finding the Best Place to Work, Live and Prosper in the 1990's and Beyond, by Dr. John Tepper Marlin, explores the job and living options for the next decade and into the next century. This consumer guide and handbook, written by one of the world's experts on cities, selects and features forty-six American cities and metropolitan areas. ($13.95 paper, $24.95 cloth)

THE CONFIDENCE FACTOR: How Self-Esteem Can Change Your Life, by Dr. Judith Briles, is based on a nationwide survey of six thousand men and women. Briles explores why women so often feel a lack of self-confidence and have a poor opinion of themselves. She offers step-by-step advice on becoming the person you want to be. ($9.95 paper, $18.95 cloth)

THE DOLLARS AND SENSE OF DIVORCE, by Dr. Judith Briles, is the first book to combine practical tips on overcoming the legal hurdles by planning finances before, during, and after divorce. ($10.95 paper)

THE ENVIRONMENTAL GARDENER: The Solution to Pollution for Lawns and Gardens, by Laurence Sombke, focuses on what each of us can do to protect our endangered plant life. A practical sourcebook and shopping guide. ($8.95 paper)

HERITAGE: The Making of an American Family, by Dr. Robert Pamplin, Jr., traces the phenomenal history of the Pamplin family from the Crusades to an eye-opening account of how they built one of the largest private fortunes in the United States. Heritage is an inspiring paradigm for achievement based on a strong belief in God and integrity. ($24.95, hardbound; $12.95 paperbound)

LIFETIME EMPLOYABILITY: How to Become Indispensable, by Carole Hyatt is both a guide through the mysteries of the business universe brought down to earth and a handbook to help you evaluate your attitudes, your skills, and your goals. Through expert advice and interviews of nearly 200 men and women whose lives have changed because their jobs or goals shifted, Lifetime Employability is designed to increase your staying power in today's down-sized economy. ($12.95 paper)

THE LIVING HEART BRAND NAME SHOPPER'S GUIDE, by Michael F. DeBakey, M.D., Antonio M. Gotto, Jr., M.D., D.Phil., Lynne W. Scott, M.A., R.D./L.D., and John P. Foreyt, Ph.D., lists brand-name supermarket products that are low in fat, saturated fatty acids, and cholesterol. ($12.50 paper)

THE LOYALTY FACTOR: Building Trust in Today's Workplace, by Carol Kinsey Goman, Ph.D., offers techniques for restoring commitment and loyalty in the workplace. ($9.95 paper)

MANAGING YOUR CHILD'S DIABETES, by Robert Wood Johnson IV, Sale Johnson, Casey Johnson, and Susan Kleinman, brings help to families trying to understand diabetes and control its effects. ($10.95 paper)

MANN FOR ALL SEASONS: Wit and Wisdom from The Washington Post's Judy Mann, by Judy Mann, shows the columnist at her best as she writes about women, families, and the impact and politics of the women's revolution. ($9.95 paper, $19.95 cloth)

OUT THE ORGANIZATION: New Career Opportunities for the 1990's, by Robert and Madeleine Swain, is written for the millions of Americans whose jobs are no longer safe, whose companies are not loyal, and who face futures of uncertainty. it gives advice on finding a new job or starting your own business. ($12.95 paper)

POSITIVELY OUTRAGEOUS SERVICE: New and Easy Ways to Win Customers for Life, by T. Scott Gross, identifies what the consumers of the nineties really want and how businesses can develop effective marketing strategies to answer those needs. ($14.95)

THE PREGNANCY AND MOTHERHOOD DIARY: Planning the First Year of Your Second Career, by Susan Schiffer Stautberg, is the first and only undated appointment diary that shows how to manage pregnancy and career. ($12.95 spiralbound)

PRELUDE TO SURRENDER: The Pamplin Family and the Siege of Petersburg, by Dr. Robert Pamplin, Jr., offers an exciting and moving narrative, interspersed with facts, of the American Civil War and the ten-month siege and battles of Petersburg, Virginia, as seen through the eyes of Dr. Pamplin's ancestors, the Boisseau family. ($10.95 hardbound)

REAL LIFE 101: The Graduate's Guide to Survival, by Susan Kleinman, supplies welcome advice to those facing "real life" for the first time, focusing on work, money, health, and how to deal with freedom and responsibility. ($9.95 paper)

SIDE-BY-SIDE STRATEGIES: How Two-Career Couples Can Thrive in the Nineties, by Jane Hershey Cuozzo and S. Diane Graham, describes how two-career couples can learn the difference between competing with a spouse and becoming a supportive power partner. Published in hardcover as Power Partners. ($10.95 paper, $19.95 cloth)

STEP FORWARD: Sexual Harassment in the Workplace, What You Need to Know, by Susan L. Webb, presents the facts for identifying the tell-tale signs of sexual harassment on the job, and how to deal with it. ($9.95 paper)

TAKING CONTROL OF YOUR LIFE: The Secrets of Successful Enterprising Women, by Gail Blanke and Kathleen Walas, is based on the authors' professional experience with Avon Products' Women of Enterprise Awards, given each year to outstanding women entrepreneurs. The authors offer a specific plan to help women gain control over their lives, and include business tips and quizzes as well as beauty and lifestyle information. ($17.95 cloth)

TWENTYSOMETHING: Managing and Motivating Today's New Work Force, by Lawrence J. Bradford, Ph.D., and Claire Raines, M.A., examines the work orientation of the younger generation, offering managers in businesses of all kinds a practical guide to better understand and supervise their young employees. ($22.95 cloth)

YOUR HEALTHY BODY, YOUR HEALTHY LIFE: How to Take Control of Your Medical Destiny, by Donald B. Louria, M.D., provides precise advice and strategies that will help you to live a long and healthy life. Learn also about nutrition, exercise, vitamins, and medication, as well as how to control risk factors for major diseases. Revised and updated. ($12.95 paper)

MasterMedia launches The Heritage Imprint—books that speak of courage, integrity and bouncing back from defeat. For the millions of Americans seeking greater purpose and meaning in their lives in difficult times, here are volumes of inspiration, solace and spiritual support.

The Heritage Imprint books will be supported by MasterMedia's full-service speakers' bureau, authors' media and lecture tours, syndicated radio interviews, national and co-op advertising and publicity.

Journey Toward Forgiveness: Finding Your Way Home
BettyClare Moffatt, M.A., best-selling author of *Soulwork* and many other books.

Discover the difference forgiveness makes in your world. Learn to overcome anger, fear and resentment and live "in ever-increasing joy and satisfaction and wonder." Step-by-step guidelines to forgiveness, meditation and prayer, action, healing and change. [$11.95, *Journey Toward Forgiveness: Finding Your Way Home* . Hardbound ISBN 1-57101-050-5, October.]

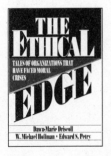

The Ethical Edge:
Tales of Organizations That Have Faced
Moral Crises.
Dawn Marie Driscoll, W. Michael Hoffman, Edward S. Petry, associated with The Center for Business Ethics at Bentley College.

The authors link the current search for meaning and values in life with stories of corporate turnarounds. Now read about organizations that have recovered from moral crises—the tough lessons they've learned, ethical structures they've put in place to ensure a solid future. If every employee followed the mission of the book, America's companies would clearly have not only a moral edge, but a competitive edge. [$24.95, The Ethical Edge: Tales of Organizations That Have Faced Moral Crises. Hardbound ISBN 1-57101-051-3, February.]

American Heroes: Their Lives. Their Values. Their Beliefs
Dr. Robert B. Pamplin, Jr., with Gary K. Eisler

Courage. Integrity. Compassion. The qualities of the hero still live in American men and women today — even in a world which can appear disillusioned. Share their stories of outstanding achievements. Discover the values that guide their lives and give courage to all of us. And learn some startling facts about what Americans really think of today's heroes, as revealed in a pioneering coast-to-coast survey.

Dr. Robert B. Pamplin, Jr. is a member of the Forbes 400, has been awarded numerous honorary degrees and has written twelve books. [$18.95, *American Heroes: Their Lives. Their Values. Their Beliefs.*. Hardbound ISBN 1-57101-010-6, late June.]

Heritage: The Making of an American Family
Dr. Robert B. Pamplin, Jr., with Gary K. Eisler, Jeff Sengstack and John Domini.
Foreward by Dr. Norman Vincent Peale.

Fascinating saga of the Pamplin family, which has built one of the largest private fortunes in America. From the Crusades to today's multimillion-dollar corporation run by the author and his father, longtime head of the Georgia-Pacific Corporation. [$12.95, *Heritage: The Making of an American Family*. Hardbound ISBN 1-57101-021-1, October.]

Prelude to Surrender: The Pamplin Family and the Siege of Petersburg
Dr. Robert B. Pamplin, Jr., with Gary K. Eisler, Jeff Sengstack and John Domini.

"The special value of the family saga portrayed [here] lies not only in its engrossing tale of the remarkable Boisseau clan, but also in the insights shared when individual tales intersect with larger events" —Noah Andre Trudeau, Civil War Historian. The author's ancestral home was taken over by the Conferderacy for use as a hospital and as a defensive position. It is now the Pamplin Park Civil War Site. [$12.95, *Prelude to Surrender* Hardbound ISBN 1-57101-049-1, September.]